HOWELLS' TRAVELS
TOWARD ART

HOWELLS' TRAVELS TOWARD ART

James L. Dean

Albuquerque
UNIVERSITY OF NEW MEXICO PRESS

TO THE MEMORY OF MY FATHER
WARREN H. DEAN

CONTENTS

1

TOWARD A THEORY OF
TRAVEL WRITING

Each genre, as it grows, establishes its own dimensions and possibilities for creative expression. W. H. Auden admirably suggests some of the problems and possibilities of travel writing in his prefatory essay to Henry James' *The American Scene:* "of all possible subjects, travel is the most difficult for an artist, as it is the easiest for a journalist. For the latter, the interesting event is the new, the extraordinary, the comic, the shocking, and all that the peripatetic journalist requires is a flair for being on the spot where and when such events happen—the rest is merely passive typewriter thumping; meaning, relation, importance, are not his quarry. The artist, on the other hand, is deprived of his most treasured liberty, the freedom to invent; successfully to extract importance from historical personal events without ever departing from them, free only to select and never to modify or to add, calls for imagination of a very high order."[1]

W. D. Howells' travel literature, at its best, demonstrates this kind of imagination. Unfortunately, no very sustained nor systematic study has been undertaken to assess the quality of this imagination or to determine the general practices and principles which affect the value of travel writing as a literary form. Though I will focus primarily upon

Howells' travel writing in this study, I will consider some theoretical principles which have relevance to the genre as a whole. I will also discuss some problems of technique peculiar to the genre and demonstrate how Howells sought to solve them.

Howells encountered problems of technique from the beginning of his career. His experience as an author and a reviewer of travel books for the *Atlantic Monthly* led him toward several worthwhile conclusions about the limitations and artistic possibilities of the genre. Of those conclusions he reached, the following are significant: The narrator must be both vital and consistent. The angle of vision counts for much more than new material. By effective use of humor and irony, the artist can counter the sterilities of conventional treatment, where style, feeling, choice of picturesque detail, jokes, and rhapsodies about art drearily conform to expectation. He can not easily resolve the moral, philosophical, and aesthetic problems posed by Europe's long history and wealth of art. He must confront them, however, and devise techniques to handle them. I will consider the implications arising from these general conclusions in more detail, but first I would like to examine some aspects of the confrontation of American and European values, since this confrontation notably influences the technical resources the artist brings to bear on the issues.

American writers frequently have expressed ambivalent attitudes about the Old and New Worlds. Cushing Strout rightly maintains in *The American Image of the Old World* that an acute necessity for reconciling this ambivalence existed in all major American writers of the nineteenth century, from Cooper to James; all were fascinated by the American-European conflict which, Strout suggests, had mythic proportions and multiple implications: "The dream of a primitive innocent New World was thus brought into contact with the facts of a complex sophisticated society, and the encounter, unsettling to American poise, fostered the ambiguity which was to mark serious American literature in the nineteenth century."[2]

American travel literature, as much as its fiction, displays this ambiguity. Howells' reviews indicate that he found it in the accounts of others, and his readers easily perceive it in his own work. Like

many Americans when first in Europe, he had strong convictions of
the moral superiority of American life, yet his years in Venice as
American consul made him increasingly sensitive to the values of
European culture. Olov Fryckstedt has convincingly demonstrated
how mixed Howells' feelings were about Europe, particularly during
his first year in Venice; in his letters, on the one hand, he would
"extol America and debunk Europe, and on the other he would describe the beauty and picturesqueness of its [Europe's] cities and
scenery."[3] Howells achieved a more balanced perspective in later
years, but his early uneasiness led him to engage in romantic postur-
ing, sweeping cultural indictments, and self-conscious demonstra-
tions of literary style and poetic feeling. In an 1867 review Howells
ironically enough castigates W. Pembroke Fetridge, author of *Harper's Handbook,* for committing sins quite similar to some Howells
himself committed a few years before. Though more guilty of chauvin-
ism and cultural boorishness, Fetridge, no less than Howells, felt im-
pelled to explain Europe and justify America. That he abysmally
failed to do so indicates the complexity of the issue as much as it
points to his prejudicial attitudes.

If nothing else, the "personal flavor and feeling so unusually strong"[4]
which Fetridge imparts to his volume causes Howells seriously to
consider the problem of the function of the narrator in a travel account.
A travel book with an oppressive personal cast has affinities with con-
fessional literature—though, to be sure, the traveler's confession is
unconscious. Yet a book must reveal the character of the writer to
some extent; Howells "likes to find a man as well as an author in a
book."[5] A vivid and forcible narrator is an asset, particularly if the
narrator does not indiscriminately take duties upon himself which
more properly belong to the philosopher, the poet, the historian, and
the comic.

Howells learned that consistency in point of view is instrumental
in creating unity of effect. He also recognized the difficulty the narrator has in being always an active consciousness and unifying center
—especially since the material of travel appears fragmentary and lacks
apparent significance. Only a few writers, Howells finds, are aware of

the necessity of creating a consistent, yet flexible narrative viewpoint. He sees advantages in a restricted point of view and a narrow range of facts, for within these limitations a good writer can move with enough imaginative freedom to create "a whole world of character, of experience, of feeling."[6] Howells' ideal narrator is one who can suggest complexity and significance as well as record surface phenomena, preserve a balance between himself and the facts observed, and advance general conclusions based on his observations. Such tasks demand great technical facility as well as "imagination of a very high order."

Howells recognizes that poetic vision can render a truth which exists beyond the facts, statistics, and generalizations based on them. A writer's angle of vision signifies more than what is seen: the writer who attempts to be definitive sees less than he should because he considers the ends more than the means. Howells also inclines to see poetic vision as superior to scientific vision; observation and recording of facts without insight into their implications strike him as futile. Ideally, Howells suggests, an unscientific travel account can reveal "something of the grace and freedom and keen mental insight which we require in a work of fiction."[7]

Because he desires freshness of vision, he often bridles at the tiresome repetition of well-known facts, emotions, scenes, and conditions. No more satisfactory are accounts which are primarily subjective in nature. The writer must see significance beyond the merely personal. Howells' reaction against sentimentality stems from his belief in the necessity of clear vision. The sentimental is pernicious because it distorts reality: The traveler sees through a colored glass. And when one can not see, he can always resort to the conventions of sentiment—substitute an expected feeling for a truly felt one (or lack of a felt one) or paste a feeling over a fact. Sentiment, when overused, becomes a kind of emotional editorializing.

Howells finds the traveler who sees only conventionally as distressing as the one who misses Europe altogether, as Fetridge appears to have done. Because he came to recognize the dangers to the writer of seeing only what conventions have taught one to see, Howells suggests the need for constant examination of beliefs in light of new experiences and contrasting viewpoints. The conventional takes many forms; at its most damning it suggests that a writer has principally seen only what he has read. If an innocent on tour, he more often than not finds himself tied to his guidebook; if more experienced, he usually finds a formula which satisfies him, and hopefully, his readers. In either case he misses the sense of personal discovery, the excitement of mental or emotional adventure.

After the Civil War, the number of travelers going to Europe greatly increased, and the number of travel books increased accordingly. As books proliferated the possibilities of treating new scenes and unusual characters decreased. Interest in the new scene quickly fades after it has been seen and described several times; the glories of its obvious differences and idiosyncrasies once or twice culled, the writer may no longer market its externals. In 1868 Howells observed that "the difficulty of writing home from Europe anything that is worth reading does not seem to affect the production of foreign letters, or the volumes of travel growing out of them."[8] Like Auden, Howells values sensibility above novelty. Novelty in observable objects counts for little with the artist; as Howells significantly states, "The freshness must be all in the spirit with which he looks at things; the variety in the ideas and associations which they evoke in him."[9]

Humor—and many manifestations appear in American travel books written during Howells' lifetime—often serves as a conventional device of the writer. A penchant for the jest, if we judge by Howells' interest in the matter, was a particularly virulent national habit. Correctly used, however, humor can be an invaluable tool of the artist.

The acknowledged ambivalence of the sensitive American writer about cultural and moral values creates unique possibilities for humor, a fact Howells apparently grasped instinctively. This humor, in turn, assists in clarifying the particular directions and nature of the ambivalence. The incongruities between the conventionally reported and the freshly observed, between the sentimental and the real, the ideal and the pragmatic, the artistic and the utilitarian, and the moral and the expedient—all these, if examined thoroughly, reveal something about the complex problems facing the American in Europe. Denied a rich culture and tradition by historical circumstance, the American finds himself adrift. He can not willingly accept Europe's substantial, if questionable (for the American), social values, but on the other hand he can not fully commit all of his trusts to the future. When he finds himself beset by such complex problems, humor becomes a means of ensuring some kind of stability of perspective and a way of balancing opposite or conflicting values. It allows him simultaneously to possess and dismiss.

Alexis de Tocqueville finds little evidence of humor in Americans, but more perceptively remarks: "among democratic nations the existence of man is more complex; the same mind will almost always embrace several objects at once, and these objects are frequently wholly foreign to each other. As it can not know them all well, the mind is readily satisfied with imperfect notions of each."[10] Tocqueville could not know what Howells discovers; entertaining "imperfect notions" simultaneously does not necessarily imply superficiality, for the "imperfectness" may be counterbalanced by the complexity of the perspective which entertains them. American humor, because it can reflect this complexity, may fill the gap between multiple foreign objects, or arbitrate between them. A flexible, complex narrator who is very much aware of how he sees, if not certain of the significance of what he sees, can provide some stability in a mental environment characterized by flux.

Howells realizes that because humor is Janus-faced, it can effectively criticize at the same time it induces laughter. If judiciously employed, it can reveal much about national shortcomings. But more significantly, Howells maintains that humor in the travel book must be an integral part of a larger intention—it should reflect the writer's vision of reality more than his desire to amuse.

Howells' irony, as much as his humor, functions critically as part of a larger intention. As a device in travel literature irony has several obvious advantages over didactic statement. As a double-edged device it affords the writer two ways of seeing something, neither of which need be definitive; it is, in a sense, a device of the open end, and thus particularly suited to the "realist." Irony accords the writer greater flexibility—he may be ironic both about himself and about what he observes. Finally, it provides a means for balancing between contingency and irresolution on one hand and fixed notions and stated values on the other.

Irony and humor can not, of course, be considered apart from style, and Howells often concerns himself with matters of style. He has stylistic standards he would like to see observed by more travel writers. He advocates simplicity and naturalness (not easily come by), grace (which suggests a distrust of rigid rhetorical patterning), sincerity, vigor, and economy. Howells also prefers a colloquial style to one characterized by finish and wit, for the former better depicts the commonplace realities encountered during travel. Moreover, it serves as an antidote to excessive poetic enthusiasm, artificiality, and imitative qualities.

Still to be resolved is the problem of Howells' aesthetic sensitivity. Nathalia Wright concludes that Howells' accounts of his early European experience show him possessing "slight aesthetic sense," not to mention a "Puritanically moral view" and little "interest in the past."[11] On the other hand, Clara Kirk, in *W. D. Howells and Art in His Time*, offers quite different conclusions; she finds Howells receptive to aesthetic values and original in his criticism of art.[12]

No matter what conclusions one reaches about Howells' aesthetic sensibility, in a sense they are beside the point—at least beside the point as Howells sees it. Howells never presumes to explain just what constitutes aesthetic sensibility. His concern is quite different. Just as he attempts to show his readers the advantages of looking at the world unsentimentally, so does he wish to show them the benefits of approaching art honestly. He feels that the viewer who depends upon expert or traditional judgments sees only what he has been prepared to see. Early in his life Howells praised Hawthorne for looking "with simple dislike upon the work he sees, untouched by the traditional admiration of all ages and nations."[13]

Howells criticizes affectation in judgments about art, and approaches the problem of art criticism reluctantly because of an aversion to technical terminology. He refuses to discuss the intention of the artist, for example, and argues that language is inadequate for the task of describing the qualities found in architecture, sculpture, and painting. The strain of anti-intellectualism evident in Howells' criticism of art stems from his belief that the "truths" of art can be sensed intuitively. He also believes that repeated viewing of a work adds to an appreciation of it, for one's feelings are educable. In his distrust of tradition and authority Howells resembles somewhat Tocqueville's American who seeks "the reason of things for oneself, and in oneself alone."[14] He realizes, however, that one does more than merely discover "the reason of things for oneself" in art; one also discovers the closeness of his ties with humanity.

Howells' attitudes toward history and its place in the travel book can be assessed no more easily than his attitudes about art. Often these attitudes are ambivalent. In general, he feels that the travel writer is obliged to give the reader some history, but a lively and interesting history. Because he values character above events, he primarily sees history as a means of revealing and illustrating character. The past, he suggests, must not be studied for its own sake but for the sake of making the present more intelligible.

Sometimes, of course, the past fails to cooperate with the writer. It remains enigmatic, or terribly disquieting in its implications about human cruelty and frailty, or irrelevant, or even incomprehensible. Late in his life Howells admits that he has always found history a baffling study, and his attitudes about it vary from year to year, even from paragraph to paragraph. At times he abhors the past, at others he suggests that study of it is futile, and at yet others he demonstrates an intense interest in its possible values and lessons. Howells' attitudes about the past are complex. Italy's past proves more difficult than England's for him to come to terms with, and it is in his English travel books that he most skillfully integrates historical material. This he primarily does by utilizing such techniques of indirection as image clusters and impressionism to suggest the rich texture of English civilization.

Howells' travels are outwardly uneventful, inwardly eventful.

Howells proves himself an uncommonly good writer of travel literature, for it is his unique talent to find new adventure in old places, to discover the extraordinary in the ordinary, and to impart to the common and incidental the luster of art. Those things Auden asks of travel writing—meaning, relation, and importance—are certainly evident in Howells' books of travel. Howells does more than practice the craft of travel writing; he demonstrates that he knows much about the theory underlying his practice. By considering such matters as vision, role of the narrator, function of irony and humor, appropriate style, and use of art and history in a travel account, he convincingly shows his awareness of the necessities of his craft and the value of travel literature as a means of revelation and discovery.

NOTES

1. W. H. Auden, ed. *The American Scene*, by Henry James (New York, 1946), p. v.

2. Cushing Strout, *The American Image of the Old World* (New York, 1963), p. 86.

3. Olov W. Fryckstedt, *In Quest of America: A Study of Howells' Early Development as a Novelist* (Upsala, Sweden, 1958), p. 37.

4. W. D. Howells [Review of W. Pembroke Fetridge's *Harper's Hand-Book for Travellers in Europe and the East*], *Atlantic Monthly*, XIX (March 1867), 382.

5. [Review of John Hay's *Castilian Days*], *Atlantic Monthly*, XXVIII (November 1871), 637.

6. [Review of Richard Henry Dana's *Two Years Before the Mast*], *Atlantic Monthly*, XXIV (August 1869), 259.

7. [Review of Bayard Taylor's *By-Ways of Europe*], *Atlantic Monthly*, XXIII (June 1869), 764.

8. [Review of Henry W. Bellows' *The Old World in its New Face: Impressions of Europe in 1867-68*], *Atlantic Monthly*, XXII (July 1868), 127.

9. [Review of Warner's *Mummies and Moslems*], *Atlantic Monthly*, XXXVIII (July 1876), 108.

10. Alexis de Tocqueville, *Democracy in America*, 2 vols. (New York, 1962), II, 234.

11. Nathalia Wright, *American Novelists in Italy* (Philadelphia, 1965), p. 171.

12. Clara Marburg Kirk, *W. D. Howells and Art in His Time* (New Brunswick, N.J., 1965), p. 31.

13. W. D. Howells [Review of Nathaniel Hawthorne's *Italian Note-Books*], *Atlantic Monthly*, XXIX (May 1872), 624.

14. Tocqueville, p. 3.

2

CONVENTION AND ORIGINALITY:
ISSUES AND DIRECTIONS

Henry James praised *Venetian Life* (1866) and *Italian Journeys* (1867) when he reviewed the latter for the *North American Review*. The two travel books possess, says James, a "perfection" in charm of style and construction; moreover, "they belong to literature and to the centre and core of it,—the region where men think and feel, and one may almost say breathe in, good prose, and where the classics stand on guard."[1] James' pleasure was shared by many nineteenth-century readers. *Venetian Life* especially received favorable critical attention; and of all Howells' travel books it has most consistently remained in critical and public view.

While sharing James' enthusiasm for the two books, one can still suggest that they have their limitations. Both *Italian Journeys* and *Venetian Life* are as notable for unresolved problems and partial failures as for successes. The qualifications Howells expresses about *Venetian Life* in the revised 1907 edition may be in part explained by the reservations that authors sometimes have when looking back on first successes; however, he also writes from a more mature perspective and with an increased awareness of the possibilities of the genre.

For a reader a hundred years removed from Howells, the conflict between his desire to be original and his dependence upon traditional modes of expression and form vividly suggests the personal, cultural, and artistic dilemmas he faced in Italy. An examination of this conflict is profitable on several counts: it is a means of clarifying and focusing upon the issue of ambivalence in the American in Europe; it points to the transitional nature of the travel books; it assists in accounting for stylistic and tonal inconsistencies, as well as pointing to problems of technique which will have to be faced in future travel books; and finally the examination sheds light on the ambivalent attitudes about the art and history which constantly concerned Howells while in Italy.

Howells' primary claim to originality lies in his description of the "real" Venice and Italy. He slights palaces and famous works of art for the everyday and the common; he debunks such writers as Byron for falsifying material which deserves faithful representation. For the critic, however, more substantial conclusions lie beyond the limited issue of his choice of material. While much testifies to the artistic promise of these early books, one can not justifiably ignore Howells' failure to find a completely adequate form and voice. His limitations, and the probable reasons for them, will be the concern of this chapter.

The problems of technique Howells faced can be stated more precisely if one knows something of the values and perspectives he brought to the Italian scene. His professed reliance upon his own "average experience"[2] rather than upon the conventions of experience indicates a typical American reluctance to accept the validity of historically established values. On the other hand, there is a difference between what he professes and what he practices. His inexperience forces him to depend, more often than he admits, upon conventional attitudes and approved literary practices. In turn, his inability to employ a consistent narrative voice leads to considerable unevenness in his work.

Noticeable and surprising shifts occur in tone and point of view. The readers of Howells' time evidently ignored or were unconcerned with the issue of tonal consistency, though one perceptive American reviewer did notice it. Moncure Conway, reviewing for the British

Fortnightly Review, found unexpected evidence of sentimentality in some passages; it was especially unexpected in light of Howells' previously demonstrated ability as a "serious, careful writer."[3] A later critic, George Carrington, maintains that the complexities of point of view in *Venetian Life* make it "more than just another piece of debunking like *The Innocents Abroad*."[4] While Carrington's flat rejection of Twain's amusing adventures is suspect, he convincingly contends that the section in *Venetian Life* entitled "A Daybreak Ramble" illustrates an intricate and complex narrative perspective. He also maintains that Howells recognized "the significance that ordinary material can acquire when seen from a novel point of view."[5]

The chapter's vividness does arise from the imaginative interplay between the observer and the material: the narrator finds something "elephantine" about a dog only a few inches high and feels "colossal" when patting its head (p. 140). Such a novel perspective, however, does not appear frequently in *Venetian Life,* and in many ways Howells follows conventions already established for the travel book. As Carrington notes, "a large part of *Venetian Life* is straight description and narration of the sort one would expect to find in any midnineteenth century travel book, e.g., the descriptive set-piece, the philosophical rumination, the historic summary of Venetian trade,"[6] while Fryckstedt suggests that Howells depends on other writers because of his desire to succeed in literature.[7]

These two impulses toward experimentation and toward success and acceptance further complicate the conflict between self-reliance and the use of tradition. Yet at his most effective Howells simultaneously utilizes and criticizes a convention; he also creates a more complex perspective. He does not always do so, as the unevenness of the work attests. Howells resembles Mark Twain in *The Innocents Abroad,* who, according to Henry Nash Smith, vacillates between ironic or humorous undercutting and serious presentation of rhetorical or "poetic" passages.[8]

Howells has not yet surrendered his desire to be a serious poet. A description of snow on St. Mark's Church in Venice can only be termed unabashedly rhapsodic:

The tender snow had compassionated the beautiful edifice for all
the wrongs of time, and so hid the strains and ugliness of decay
that it looked as if just from the hand of the builder,—or better
said, just from the brain of the architect. There was a marvelous
freshness in the colors of the mosaics in the great arches of the
facade, and all that gracious harmony into which the temple rises,
of marble scrolls and leafy exuberance airily supporting the
statues of the saints, as a hundred times etherealized by the purity
and whiteness of the drifting flakes. The snow lay lightly on the
golden globes that tremble like peacock-crests above the vast
domes, and plumed them with softest white; it robed the saints in
ermine, and it danced over all its work, as if exulting in its
beauty. . . . (pp. 52-53)

The conventional rhapsodizer, with his battery of lush adjectives and
his penchant for rhetorical efflorescence, is unhappily dominant.
Such language is by no means unusual in *Venetian Life* (fewer
flourishes appear in *Italian Journeys*), nor does Howells reveal any
awareness of such excess. I doubt if he had in mind his own dictum
that "only those travelers who invent in cold blood their impressions
of memorable places ever have remarkable impressions to record" (p.
223).

He does have some suspicions about the efficacy of such writing in
the following description of the church of Santa Maria dell' Orto. He
catches a rhapsodic impulse in mid-paragraph and neatly reverses it:
"The facade is exquisite, and has two Gothic windows of that religious
and heavenly beauty which pains the heart with its inexhaustible
richness. One longed to fall down on the space of green turf before
the church, now bathed in the soft October sunshine, and recant
these happy, commonplace centuries of heresy, and have back again
the good old believing days of bigotry, and superstition, and roasting,
and racking, if only to have once more the men who dreamed those
windows out of their faith and piety (if they did, which I doubt), and
made them with their patient, reverent hands (if their hands were
reverent, which I doubt)" (pp. 212-13). The sharp contrast between

reverence and irreverence has the effect of making the reaction to the scene more important than the scene itself; one may have an impulse to rhapsodize and a suspicion of its appropriateness at the same time. Howells' doubt permits a suspension of belief—which in turn frees him and the reader from the necessity of voicing or hearing an authoritative, absolute, or conventional sentiment expressed about art, morality, national character, or whatever. This suspension certainly does not constitute a rejection of either the artists or of what they have created. More than anything the passage suggests the author's strong moral bias.

The conflict between the moralist and the artist invests *Venetian Life* with more than ordinary significance, for in Howells' desire to affirm the superiority of American ethics, and in his increasing, if reluctant, recognition of the undeniable beauties and richness of European culture, he is a representative American facing a national predicament. He sometimes succeeds in minimizing the tension in this conflict by projecting himself into it as an intimate narrator. The personal voice and even the biases of this narrator help create unity, relevance, and significance in the absence of known truths about a strange and fascinating civilization. As a general rule, when an episode or scene seems flat, rhapsodic, dogmatically assertive, or when it is tediously detailed (as the section on Venetian commerce is), the presence of the intimate narrator diminishes and a somewhat more general standard voice appears.

This second voice which jars so rudely against one's expectations of freshness and originality also appears in the generally more subdued and iconoclastic *Italian Journeys*. One wishes a skeptical and personal voice had been used, for example, in this adulatory address directed at Gothic architecture: "O beloved beauty of aspiring arches, of slender and clustered columns, of flowering capitals and window-traceries, of many carven breadths and heights, wherein all Nature breathes and blossoms again! There is neither Greek perfection, nor winning Byzantine languor, nor insolent Renaissance opulence, which may compare with this loveliness of yours!"[9] The loveliness of the Gothic is less in question than the voice which declaims it. The proclivity of the narrator to speak for heaven, nature, and man renders his judgments questionable; one regrets the subordination of personal uniqueness and imagination, the precedence given a voice which so easily lifts experience to metaphysical regions.

Howells complains in *Italian Journeys* that "all moisture of romance and adventure has been well nigh sucked out of travel in Italy" (p. 157), but he does not always refuse to fill in gaps with rhapsodic effusions, remarkable only in the degree to which sense is sacrificed to sound and sentiment. On the other hand, when he creates his best effects, as in the section entitled "Forza Maggiore," which James praises as a "masterpiece of light writing,"[10] little of the conventional language of travel obtrudes itself. The "adventure" is slight and hardly romantic in its implications, but is charming and economical in its expression. In the "adventure" Howells writes of no more remarkable an occurrence than the upending of a diligence in a flooded area. During the attempt to rescue certain items, the attention of the narrator fastens upon a hat:

> It was of the sort called in Italian as in English slang a stove-pipe (*canna*), and having been made in Italy, it was of course too large for its wearer. It had never been anything but a horror and reproach to him, and he was now inexpressibly delighted to see it steal out of diligence in company with one of the red-leather cushions, and glide darkly down the flood. It nodded and nodded to the cushion with a super-human tenderness and elegance, and had a preposterous air of whispering, as it drifted out of sight,—
>
> > "It may be we shall reach the Happy Isles,—
> > It may be that the gulfs shall wash us down."
>
> The romantic interest of this episode had hardly died away, when our adventure acquired an idyllic flavor from the appearance on the scene of four peasants in an ox-cart. (pp. 191-92)

Such an unlikely romance—embellished with the proper diction of romance ("whispering," "nodded," "glide darkly," "tenderness," "ele-

gance")—creates a fine comic effect. When the reader recognizes that
the hat nobly recites two heroic lines from Tennyson's *Ulysses,* he
likes the effect even better. In such a minor disaster as this the surface action signifies little; significance resides in the reactions of the
narrator and in the parody of romantic diction.

One can not predict with accuracy the voice or the language which
Howells may use. Any particular episode or description is as apt to
end facetiously or ironically as seriously. Little evidence of parody
appears in the most obviously rhetorical or conventional accounts.
Howells appears to fashion, on the one hand, a voice which expresses
his audience's tastes and proprieties; on the other he speaks brashly
and personally, flaunting or ironically treating these same proprieties.
In *Italian Journeys* he can seriously question the inexperienced American's "desire to be perfectly up in critical appreciation of the arts,
and to approach the great works in the spirit of the connoisseur" (p.
166), but he can also be thoroughly superior in the standard preference for American sanitation, living conditions, and character.

His description of some streets near the Theater of Pompey in Rome
certainly illustrates such a preference: "In the rascal streets in the
neighborhood of the most august ruins, the people turn around to stare
at the stranger as he passes them; they are all dirty, and his decency
must be no less a surprise to them than the neatness of the French
soldiers amid all the filth is a puzzle to him" (p. 162). Even when
being iconoclastic, Howells occasionally yields to the pressures of saying something appropriate. When he describes Rome as "first and
last hideous" (p. 152), he does not yield. But when discussing Roman
fever he modulates his criticism to some extent, reporting with ironic
overtones, that he, alas, "caught the Roman fever—the longing that
burns one who has once been in Rome to go again—that will not be
cured by all the cool contemptuous things he may think or say of the
Eternal City; that fills him with fond memories of its fascination, and
makes it forever desired" (p. 171).

The reader is not sure whether Howells dismisses Roman fever as
mere romantic nonsense—though obviously his enthusiasm for "hideous" Rome is slight since the ambiguity in his statement makes any

final judgment difficult. It also reveals the several voices which the narrator must assume. He must speak for his traveling companions, the readers, in a general way (the averageness of their experience is assumed to be much like his); in addition he must educate them from their misconceptions, and so serve as a pedagogue and sometimes as an iconoclast. But he must also speak in an intimate, unique voice, record impressions, glance into unexpected corners of experience, and look closely at the trivial and the common. The personal voice, almost without exception, has a truer ring to it.

A conflict also exists between what might be termed dramatic and editorial voices. Howells' interest in the drama appears early in *Venetian Life*; his interest in Goldoni and the Italian theater gives impetus to a natural inclination to look for the small, unobtrusive dramatic incidents of common life.[11] Yet extended dramatic encounters of the sort later found in his novels rarely occur; characters whom the narrator sees or meets are seldom portrayed as having complex motives. Nor are they extensively characterized. Yet they impart a sense of concreteness. To the degree that these characters act out their own parts in the dramatic scene and to the extent that the narrator refrains from extracting a moral judgment from the action the dramatic episodes usually succeed.

A scene in which no dialogue occurs, but which still has fine dramatic potential, appears in a chapter of *Italian Journeys* entitled "Up and Down Genoa." Howells finds "an idle, cruel crowd, amusing itself with the efforts of a blind old man to find the entrance [to a church]. He had a number of books which he desperately laid down while he ran his helpless hands over the clustered columns, and which he desperately caught up again, in fear of losing them. At other times he paused, and wildly clapsed his hands upon his eyes, or wildly threw up his arms; and then began to run to and fro again uneasily, while the crowd laughed and jeered" (p. 61). There is a suggestion of pathos, but the scene is a vivid, compelling one. Its effect, however, diminishes in the lines which follow; the narrator enters the scene and explains its import. "Doubtless," he says, "a taint of madness afflicted him; but not the less he seemed the type of a blind soul that gropes darkly about through life, to find the doorway of some divine truth and beauty,—touched by the heavenly harmonies from within, and miserably failing, amid the scornful cries and bitter glee of those who have no will but to mock aspiration" (p. 61). One wishes, perhaps cruelly, that the mad beggar had remained mad rather than serving the needs of instruction and typology.

Fortunately, Howells generally allows a dramatic scene to carry a lighter load of direct comment. A fine example appears in the treatment of a funeral. Again the diction has edges of pathos, but a fine ironic tone dominates. The narrator records the absurdities of a jovial burial crew which he and a companion follow to a cemetery. After an unceremonious rite, the narrator, his companion, and a stranger remain at the grave. Their conversation and the concluding comments by the narrator beautifully suggest the pathos and the sharp and bitter lesson learned about human indifference and the absurdity of death:

> We strangers stay behind a little, to consult with another spectator, Venetian, this.
> "Who is the dead man, signore?"
> "It is a woman, poor little thing! Dead in childbed. The baby is in there with her."
> It has been a cheerful funeral, and yet we are not in great spirits as we go back to the city.
> For my part, I do not think the cry of sea-gulls on a gloomy day is a joyous sound; and the sight of those theatrical angels, with their shameless, unfinished backs, flying off the top of the rococo facade of the church of the Jesuits, has always been a spectacle to fill me with despondency and foreboding. (*VL*, p. 327)

Throughout the scene the narrator's presence is less obtrusive than in the account of the blind beggar. The conclusions advanced in the last paragraph have no editorial cast to them. The quality of the scene derives from its indirection and from what James terms "poetic inconclusiveness."[12] Yet it is difficult to say why the two closing images seem so appropriate. They embody here a particular instance of what

James so aptly calls the "constant mute eloquence of Italian life."[13] Howells skillfully points to the pathos of the incident. He also shows an awareness of the absence of causal relationships in human affairs, of the irrevocable fact of death, and of the powerful ironies which mock man's sense of well-being. Because he lets the material speak for itself and makes the narrator's voice less direct and emphatic in its judgments (he retains the personal note), he effectively and expressively demonstrates what a sensitive writer can do with travel.

Nevertheless, when Howells' effects are unsatisfactory because of dual, or even multiple, voices, when he speaks more poetically in less consciously attempting to be a poet, when he is not the able realist he will be, questions such as these invariably arise: What in *Venetian Life* and *Italian Journeys* may be construed as prefiguring realistic practice as it is later to be defined? To what critical precepts does Howells subscribe? What conventions does he utilize in those portions of the travel books which are most obviously nonrealistic?

As early as *Italian Journeys* Howells comments that "rags of sentimentality flutter from every crag and olive-tree and orange-tree in all Italy" (p. 287), yet some of them also flutter in his own writing. On the one hand he criticizes sentimentality in other writers, and on the other he writes, without apology, passages which can only be termed sentimental. The extent of Howells' reaction against the conventions of sentimentality has been ably demonstrated in studies by Edwin Cady and Everett Carter. Cady shows that Howells came to think of sentimentality as "irresponsible emotionality," that he revolted against it, and that "his personal and social morality, much of his literary practice and much of his battle for realism stemmed from that revolt. . . ."[14] Carter finds the attack on sentimentality to be "the initial force in the development of American realism."[15] In the general interest paid to Howells' reaction against a sentimental tradition less attention has been paid his *use* of the sentimental. In these early travel books his revolt is very tentative and his realism incipient.

Howells' frequent criticism of Byron stems from his suspicion that the English poet was guilty of "irresponsible emotionality"; he prepared his emotions for a scene more than he recorded genuinely felt ones.[16] Howells feels Byron and his followers employ a "well regulated imagination" (*VL*, p. 13). Unlike these sentimental poetasters, Howells will dispense with illusions, view the material of common life and honestly report what he feels. A lighthearted illustration of his professed freedom from conventional approaches occurs early in *Venetian Life* during a visit to some famous dungeons under the Ducal Palace: "And what fables concerning these cells have not been uttered and believed! For my part, I prepared my coldest chills for their exploration, and I am not sure that before I entered their gloom some foolish and lying literature was not shaping itself in my mind, to be afterward written out as my Emotions on looking at them. I do not say now that they are calculated to enamour the unimpounded spectator with prison-life; but they are certainly far from being as bad as I hoped" (pp. 13-14).

At times Howells directly criticizes the standard practice of associationism by using the "prepared" language proper to associations for humorous or ironic effect. At a marketplace he records the following scene: "Peasants were building cabbages into pyramids; collective squashes and cucumbers were taking a picturesque shape; wreaths of garlic and garlands of onions graced the scene. All the people were clamoring at the tops of their voices; and in the midst of the tumult and confusion, resting on heaps of cabbage-leaves and garbage, men lay on their bellies sweetly sleeping" (*VL*, pp. 143-44). Here the language of prepared emotions has been made to describe objects hardly appropriate to it. "Wreaths," "garlands," and "picturesque shapes" can as well describe onions, garlic, and squash as standard "Objects of Interest" (*VL*, p. 33). These objects strike Howells as less rewarding for study than "dirty neighborhoods that reeked with unwholesome winter damps below" (*VL*, p. 33). Yet, though Howells sometimes uses "proper" language to create an ironic effect, one can not ignore those places in the narrative where he uses such language seriously.

Because of Howells' vacillations between the sentimental and the anti-sentimental, one begins to suspect that he is less interested in rejecting the sentimental tradition than in criticizing what he sees to be its sterilities and excesses. In "Our Last Year in Venice," the closing chapter of the new and enlarged edition of 1872, an explicit statement of what was intended suggests the scope of his approach to the issue of sentimentality:

> We rarely sentimentalized consciously, and still more seldom openly, about the present state of Venice as contrasted with her past glory. I am glad to say that we despised the conventional poetastery about her; but I believe that we had so far lived into sympathy with her, that, whether we realized it or not, we took the tone of her dispiritedness, and assumed a part of the common experience of loss and hopelessness. History, if you live where it was created, is a far subtler influence than you suspect; and I would not say how much Venetian history, amidst the monuments of her glory and the witnesses of her fall, had to do in secret and tacit ways with the prevailing sentiment of existence, which I now distinctly recognize to have been a melancholy one. No doubt this sentiment was deepened by very freshly added association with memorable places; and each fact, each great name and career, each strange tradition as it rose out of the past for us and shed its pale lustre upon the present, touched us with a pathos which we could neither trace nor analyze.[17]

James, it would seem, accurately judged Howells when he termed him the "very worthy successor to the author of the 'Sentimental Journey.' "[18] Yet Howells' iconoclasm, his distrust of conventional poetastery, and his avoidance of emotional excesses at least hint at an emerging realism. But the issues of realism go beyond the uses and misuses of the sentimental. Technique and structure must also be considered.

Howells employs several techniques which, when modified, become part of his mature realism. When he commends Goldoni for the "admirable fidelity of drawing and coloring" (*VL*, p. 73) in his comedies, he suggests his own interest in drama as a means of accurately and realistically presenting character and action. The number of stage metaphors and allusions to drama attests to this concern. Before the final chapter, "Ducal Mantua," was added to *Italian Journeys,* the book closed with an image of a desolate theater. The image conveys the strong, poignant feelings which arise from the constant interplay of past and present: "The gay paintings hang in shreds and tatters from the roof; dust is thick upon the seats and in the boxes, and on the leads that line the space once flooded for naval games. The poor plaster statues stand naked and forlorn amid the ruin of which they are part; and the great stage, from which the curtain has rotted away, yawns dark and empty before the empty auditorium" (pp. 319-20). Howells finds that the past, like the present, acquires significance when it can be dramatically represented.

The dramatic mode provides him with a means for portraying the pervasive conflict between illusion and reality and the ambiguities which arise from this conflict. He frequently associates the real with the dramatic; illusion and sentimentality with the melodramatic. Describing a castle of the Dukes of Ferrera he emphasizes its present shabbiness in contrast to its illustrious past. He then concludes: "The melodrama is over, friends, and now we have a play of real life, founded on fact and inculcating a moral" (*IJ*, p. 33). The "play of real life" constantly thrusts itself before Howells' vision.[19] He delights in a quarrel between two tradesmen, sympathetically presents the innocent amours of an ancient dandy, or accurately portrays the mild oppressions of a mouse-like man. The details of such dramatic scenes are not numerous, but they are usually appropriate; the inculcated moral is not oppressive.

The effectiveness of the dramatic scene depends upon the appropriateness of the facts and details used to grace it—and upon the fidelity with which they are recorded. Howells fills his scenes with human "facts." Describing landscape or architecture is not his forte; his eye is never the eye of James, which finds a scene arranging itself "as if composition were the chief end of human institutions."[20] Though Howells handles such scenes adequately, the human element speaks much more eloquently for him than any other. Art and life are not fused for him in Venice as they are for James.[21] Though Howells takes the human scene and its details for his purview, he sometimes succumbs to the picturesque. Fryckstedt maintains, with some justification, that Howells condescends to the Italians—that he treats the aesthetic values of their picturesque poverty and colorful wretchedness.[22]

Howells, however, insists that he differs markedly from most other travel writers in showing "as much as possible of the every-day life of a people whose habits are so different from our own; endeavoring to develop a just notion of their character, not only from the show-traits which strangers are most likely to see, but also from experience of such things as strangers are most likely to miss" (VL, p. 94). Yet we do find him deviating from his professed just treatment of character. He finds a beggar always sitting in the same place on a bridge and concludes that the beggar "succeeds, I believe, as the season advances, in heating the marble beneath him by firm and unswerving adhesion, and establishes a reciprocity of warmth with it. I have no reason to suppose that he ever deserts his seat for a moment during the whole winter; and indeed, it would be a vicious waste of comfort to do so" (VL, pp. 44-45). The notion is certainly an irreverent and extravagant one, and hardly humane or just. As James ironically notes, the misery inherent in such a Venetian scene "is part of the spectacle—a thorough-going devotee of local colour might consistently say it is part of the pleasure."[23] Howells, unfortunately, does not always resist the temptation to place misery in picturesque poses or make it a function of his wit, and the fidelity of his portraiture suffers. On the whole, however, he views the Italians with compassion, humor, and some measure of objectivity.

Irony and humor are the most common technical instruments he uses to create a sense of objectivity and realism. In checking an impulse to treat a fish-market as picturesque, he observes: "But a fish-market, even at Rialto, with fishermen in scarlet caps and *triglie* in sunset splendors, is only a fish-market after all: it is wet and slimy under foot, and the innumerable gigantic eels, writhing everywhere, set the soul asquirm, and soon-sated curiosity slides willingly away" (VL, p. 300). The playful alliteration and the matter-of-fact acceptance of things as they are leave little room for the picturesque.

Howells' irreverence and skepticism reflect Ohio and the West. He certainly anticipates Twain's discourteous treatment of the Old World in *The Innocents Abroad*. He sees through the shams and appearances confronting the traveler no less than Twain does. A few of his comments border on the outrageous, and in expressing them he affirms what Henry Nash Smith calls the values of the "colloquial." These values derive from the world of experience and observation; they stand in sharp relief against the ideal world of values as formulated and conventionalized by the forces of civilization.[24] In Howells these colloquial values can be seen in his common-sense approach to new experience, in a degree of anti-intellectualism, in a "native" distrust of tradition, and in a preference for the concrete, observable present to an abstract, futile past.

When Howells elaborately describes an outdated, inefficient stove which has trouble heating itself, the hyperbole in his statement has the effect of pointing to superior American technology. The practical American can be warmed by an efficient if unpicturesque stove. Howells keeps a straight face when discussing the past glories of Venetian commerce, and, in conclusion, states that "in this day our own western steamers are known to run in a heavy dew" (*VL*, p. 239). The sly boast about American commerce and the flavor of the "tall tale" indicate that Howells has a typical American suspicion that the past in Europe magnifies itself beyond its proper proportion. If the past of Europe must continually tax our belief, Howells seems to be saying, let us also tax hers by telling tales as tall.

No wonder then that in *Venetian Life* he gleefully treats such an unlikely subject as the efficiency of American pigs, or that he discusses certain unique religious practices in the same paragraph with the pigs: "In the fields, along the road, were vines and Indian corn; but instead of those effigies of humanity, doubly fearful from their wide unlikeness to any thing human, which we contrive to scare away the birds, the devout peasant-folks had here displayed on poles the instruments of the Passion of the Lord—the hammer, the cords, the nails—which at once protected and blessed the fields. But I doubt if even these would save them from the New World pigs . . ." (p. 177). America is a land of the present—in its secularity and its pigs. The elaborate circumlocution adds to the absurdity of the implied relationship between scarecrows and sacred symbols, while such extravagant sallies against superstition have the merit of wit, unhappily lacking in several of his more serious discussions of religion. His wit and humor, even in *Venetian Life,* often go beyond "fun." At its best it is, as Edwin Cady says, "a critical, often a self-critical, instrument for conveying the subtlest meanings."[25]

The hyperbolic statements throughout *Venetian Life,* and to a lesser degree those found in *Italian Journeys,* have a critical function insofar as they affirm colloquial values. The hyperbolic seems well suited to the services of such values through its affinities with burlesque, with mock-heroic language (sometimes used in these early books), and with the tall tale. Less incisive and quick than irony, less direct than sarcasm, and less intellectual and formal than satire, it nevertheless does yeoman service in establishing the "real" as worthy of consideration. It lends itself to anticlimax and allows the greatest extravagance to be stated in the calmest of voices. It combines readily with irreverence and admirably serves the "innocent" observer from America. Indeed, Howells often pleads his inexperience and naiveté in order to prepare the reader for extravagance or breaches in taste. His conclusion about Titian's painting of martyred St. Lawrence is typical. He envies the martyr, who on such a cold day is "toasting so comfortably on his grid iron" (*VL,* p. 46). At another time he judges that a famous marble drapery in the church of the Redentore is altogether "table-clothy" in appearance (*VL,* p. 46).

Other methods or devices suggesting realistic practice beyond those suggested earlier are these: cataloguing of the objects of common life, representation of reality through impressions, inconclusiveness in treating material, and selectivity in treating the facts of experience.

The catalogues Howells draws up for the reader have much less graphic detail in them than those of a novelist like Flaubert; they do differ, however, from conventional rhapsodic catalogues of palaces, objects of interest, and the True and Memorable (Howells' capitalization), which James finds happily impossible by 1892.[26] One of Howells' most effective catalogues appears in *Italian Journeys* when he describes what he terms "tumultuous" and "odd"—Neapolitan life as found in side streets. He finds a street filled "with men quarreling themselves purple over small quantities of fish—with asses braying loud and clear above their discord—with women roasting pine-cones at charcoal fires—with children in the agonies of having their hair combed—with degraded poultry and homeless dogs—with fruit stands and green groceries, and the little edifices of ecclesiastical architecture for the sale of lemonade—with wandering bag-pipers, and herds of nonchalant goats . . ." (*IJ*, p. 141). After an initial generalization Howells presents the scene without noticeable comment about its meaning. The merits of the presentation reside in the accuracy of the somewhat general observation, in the variety of the objects observed, and in the sweep of the rapidly moving eye, all of which create a sense of the immediacy of the scene. The effect of the scene depends not upon arrangement but upon the rapid progression of images—fluidity rather than fixity characterizes it.

A contrast between this effective catalogue from *Italian Journeys* and one of a street scene in *Venetian Life* reveals the increased objectivity of the narrator. Howells finds a wide thoroughfare leading to the Riva "at once insufferable and indescribable." It is, he continues, "abandoned to the poorest classes who manifest themselves, as the poorest classes are apt to do always, in groups of frowsy women, small girls carrying large babies, beggars, of course, and soldiers" (p. 291). A few lines later he describes the participants in a promenade through a garden made by Napoleon: "I do not remember to have seen here any Venetians of the better class, except on the Mondays-of-the-Garden, in September. Usually the promenaders are fishermen, Austrian corporals, loutish youth of low degree, and women too old and too poor to have anything to do. Strangers go there, and the German visitors even drink the exceptionable beer which is sold in the wooden cottage on the little hillock at the end of the Gardens. There is also a stable—where are the only horses in Venice. They are let at a florin an hour, and I do not know why the riders are always persons of the Hebrew faith. In a word, nothing can be drearier than the company in the Gardens . . ." (p. 292). At best the list suggests an awareness of class structure; at worst it reveals a peevish and aristocratic tone of voice. The slanted diction used to describe the persons diminishes the possibilities for objective appraisal. The passage shows the author's biases more than it demonstrates his critical acumen.

In the description of the Venetian street Howells sacrifices interest in action and character to self-righteous social and moral statement, and investigation to opinion. The treatment of the Neapolitan scene (in its objectivity and diminished authorial presence) points more obviously to future realistic practice. Though Howells does not use the catalogue extensively (he has little regard for quantities of details), he uses it effectively on occasion—especially to record a panoramic scene. When it serves the purposes of the moral, the picturesque, or the sentimental it is less effective. In this regard *Italian Journeys* marks a growth in technical skill over *Venetian Life*.

Howells uses the impression more often than he does the catalogue. The degree of realism suggested by his impressionism is a debatable point. Fryckstedt sees it as admirably suited for rendering the aesthetic and for preserving Howells' American ideals; however, it is not a useful instrument of realism. Moreover, the impressionistic method tends toward superficiality. Howells, Fryckstedt states, rarely attempts "to penetrate beneath the surface except in the more factual chapters at the end of the book." He writes of a "remotely observed people whom he does not know at all or with whom he has only a bare acquaintance."[27]

Howells evidently thought better of his abilities. His primary concerns are to render a scene faithfully, to give a just notion of character, and to search for the inner meanings of external objects.[28] The impression may only reflect the surfaces of life, but the trivia, the gestures, and the manners reflected have their own kind of truth—they could not be adequately rendered by more detailed or analytical means—and James's praise of the "poetic inconclusiveness" in *Italian Journeys* implies his awareness of this. The truth one sees during a given moment may disappear in the next. To be inconclusive and to rely on implication in an attempt to capture this "truth" requires some technical skill.

Howells also finds value in the undefined. His reaction to such a common object as a cat on a snowy roof illustrates this as explicitly as anything: "My black cat looked wondering upon the snow for a moment, and then ran across the roof. Nothing could have been better. Any creature less silent, or in point of movement less soothing to the eye, than a cat would have been a torture to the spirit. As it was, this little piece of action contented me so well that I left everything else out of my reverie, and could only think how deliciously the cat harmonized with the snow-covered tiles, the chimney-pot, and the dormer window. I began to long for her reappearance, but when she did come forth and repeat her manoeuvre, I ceased to have the slightest interest in the matter, and experienced only the disgust of satiety" (*VL*, p. 51). The narrator is content with the scene and the action as they are, and not especially concerned with their meaning. Howells' emphasis on the fleeting nature of the experience foreshadows the concern of future writers with techniques designed to retain the impressions of experience. Admittedly, the means Howells uses to create the impression here are not overly subtle; we are presented with a formula for an impression as much as with an impression itself. Still the passage is notable for its concern with the relationship between object and effect and the momentary and tenuous act of perception. The passage has a further implication: how one perceives an object may determine its value. By using the impression the writer frees himself from the necessity of compiling facts for purposes of demonstration, and he can affirm the legitimacy of an emotional response.

Characteristically, Howells demonstrates some ambivalence in his attitude toward the impression. It attracts him because it frees him from the strictures of fact, but he is also suspicious of it because it does so. He admits to some ignorance about Mantuan history and states that his ignorance enables him "to make out of the twilight which involved all impressions a misty and heroic picture of the Mantuan past, wherein her great men appeared with a stately and gigantic uncertainty of outline, and mixed with dim scenes of battle, intrigue, and riot, and were gone before Fact could lay her finger on any shape, and swear that it was called so, and did so and so."[29] The "dimness" and "uncertainty" of the impressions prompt Howells to wish for a few facts. When he has facts, however, he does not treat them with absolute courtesy. When he has none, he may create them, as he does for Mantua: "As I have found no explicit records of this period," he says, "I distribute to the city as her portion of the calamities, at least two sieges, one capture and sack, and a decimation by famine and pestilence."[30] In Italy, at least, distinctions between fact and fiction are blurred. Howells feels that "an Italian would rather enjoy a fiction than know a fact" (*IJ*, p. 18) and is not necessarily foolish to do so. Howells also feels the pressure of fiction on actual experience. "It is," he admits, "one of the pleasures of by-way travel in Italy, that you are everywhere introduced in character, that you become fictitious and play a part as in a novel" (*IJ*, p. 280).

The elusive nature of the past, the shifting identities of fact and fiction, and the appearances of the present may be delineated by using a method which emphasizes the narrator's response and makes it the "truth" of the matter. Howells suggests as much in a description of a landscape seen during a visit to the Villa Reale in Naples: "If I remember aright, the sun is always setting on the bay, and you cannot tell whether this sunset is cooled by the water or the water is warmed by the golden light upon it, and upon the city, and upon the soft mountain-heights around" (*IJ*, p. 81). The quaint impossibility does not vitiate the value of the impression.

Insofar as the impressions of these volumes reflect a personal voice and are instrumental in giving play to Howells' fancy and humor, they can not wholly be seen as constituting a technique of realism. But since they furnish a means of viewing life freshly, and more especially since they record elusive reality, they may be said to record the matter of experience with fidelity. The impressions of *Venetian Life* and *Italian Journeys* frequently seem whimsical, facetious, and hyperbolic; however, they do provide the critic an insight into Howells' attitudes about observation and the structure of experience.

Howells does not randomly use impressions. When James reviews *Italian Journeys* he praises Howells' craftsmanship. Howells, James notes, chooses what he wishes, neglects what he wishes, "takes things as he finds them,"[31] yet gives shape and direction to them. Such shaping makes his work superior to the "slipshod and slovenly" efforts James finds most travel accounts to be.[32] Howells displays his awareness of the need for arrangement and selection when criticizing an inept account of Mantuan history. The author of this account, it seems, has ingeniously avoided "all that might make his theme attractive."[33] It fails because he has "little in his paper to leaven statistical heaviness; and in recounting one of the most picturesque histories, he contrives to give merely a list of the events and a diagram of the scenes."[34] Howells also complains of certain Italian writers "who dig out of archives and libraries some topic of special and momentary interest and print it, unstudied and unphilosophized. Their books are material, not literature . . ." (IJ, p. 37).

Alternation and opposition of detail contribute significantly to the development of the theme of *Venetian Life*,[35] which, roughly speaking, is the constant clash between reality and illusion in Venice. If a chapter begins descriptively and rhapsodically, it will usually close with ironic undercutting or humorous anecdote. If Howells venerates or approves the past at a certain point, he will more than likely disparage it within a short span. He frequently shifts from the reverential to the ridiculous, from the fanciful to the most matter of fact, or from the impressionistic to the objective. He also uses anticlimax effectively to dramatize the conflict between expectation and actuality. Indeed, the constant frustration of the narrator's expectation is indispensable to the effect.

Such devices as anticlimax, ironic reversal, and skeptical qualification have their uses, but they do not tell the complete tale of Howells' ability to organize his material. Oscar Firkins finds the unity of *Venetian Life* comparable to that of Emerson's *English Traits*, and attributes it to the "advantage of writing a train of essays rather than a string of memoranda."[36] These essays have a unity beyond that given them by the presence of a single narrator; the effect of any single essay depends in some measure on preceding material. The connection between essays is also more than merely chronological. The essays possess in admirable degree spatial, logical, and dramatic ordering as well.

Howells' interest in the drama has been amply demonstrated, but limited attention has been paid to influences of the drama on the methods of his travel books. Nathalia Wright, for example, emphasizes the interest rather than the technical manifestations of it when she accurately states: "Italy at its most appealing was to Howells, as he suggested in his description of Venice, supremely a theatre, where the novel and the common, the particular and the universal complemented each other."[37] Technical manifestations of this interest in the theater, I feel, also exist.

The narrator, though reticent to name himself or create a specific identity for himself, serves in *Venetian Life* as the leading character in a drama of observation, impression gathering, and recording. Before his entrance onto the stage of Venice proper he presents a program, a prologue of sorts, suggesting what will follow. He sketches in the present condition of the city and provides certain necessary background information about the condition of the theater he is about to enter. Then in the second chapter, "Arrival and First Days in Venice," he enters the city by gondola. He gives his first general impressions of the city and suggests his interest in "simple, abstract humanity" (p. 35). By the third chapter, "Winter in Venice," one senses a movement from an overview to a more particular and limited perspective. The focus of the observer narrows as he looks more closely at certain physical and aesthetic objects and then at a particular seasonal condition. The geographical focus narrows even more in the next section, "Comincia Far Caldo," which mainly treats the Piazza before St. Mark's: the lagoon, shops, *caffés*, and palaces.

In subsequent chapters Howells concerns himself with such topics as the dramatic arts (opera and theater), domestic life, individual Venetians, architecture and art, villages bordering Venice, and minority groups (Armenians and Jews). He provides both variety and a panoramic view in this drama of real life; he also selects those areas of human activity which best reveal the character of the Italians. He moves from a general view of all of Venice to an extended concern with a few individual Venetians and then again toward general sociological and moral considerations in the late chapters, "Venetian Traits

and Characters" and "Society." The last chapter, "Our Last Year in
Venice," is retrospective. It serves as an epilogue, with its final look
and synthesis. Then the principal character (now with a family) de-
parts by gondola from the theater that is Venice. The illusions and
dramatic expectations of the young traveler who ironically queries,
"Is not Venice forever associated with bravoes and unexpected dagger-
thrusts?" (p. 30), are neatly balanced by the actuality of domestic
affections and an outwardly uneventful leave-taking.

Italian Journeys presents quite different problems in structuring
travel material. Howells preferred it to Venetian Life,[38] which in the
preface to an 1891 edition he termed "distinctly a youthful book"
whose faults he knew as well as those of his youth.[39] Most critics have
disagreed with his preference.[40] Generally they have stressed the thinness of the material and the lack of unity in the volume. Thinness
however, is less a problem than unevenness. Counterbalancing the
"impression of detachment, tenuity, and disparity"[41] which Firkins
notes, correctly enough, are sections and scenes which surpass nearly
anything in Venetian Life.

If Howells does not create a uniform effect in Italian Journeys the
difficulty in doing so is greater: experience has assumed a more frag-
mented aspect, thoughtful consideration of material is foreshortened by
the exigencies of travel, and a broader spectrum of social interaction,
art, and history presents itself to the viewer for appraisal. Greater
selectivity becomes a necessary and critical function. If such selectivity
seems overly rigorous (certainly Howells' treatment of Rome startles
by the sparseness of observation), one nevertheless appreciates the
more objective tone, the reduction in rhapsodies and sentimental
poses, and the improved rendering of dramatic material.

Howells was aware of the problem of unity in his material, as his
highly selective approach to his material demonstrates. Moreover, he
attempts, with limited success, to create some sort of thematic unity
for Italian Journeys. He does this primarily by frequently referring
to mutability. These references come to be a kind of motif—points
about which the material may be grouped. Not surprisingly the generally explicit statements about the impermanence of the present show

Howells' ambivalence. He inclines to reject the past, but it intrigues him because of its profound lessons about the transiency of man's institutions and individual achievements. Thus he can not wholly dismiss it.

He frequently alludes to the New World during his musings about the destructiveness of time. When visiting Capri he notes how quickly the marvels of Venice and Niagara and "all marvelously grand and lovely things make haste to prove their impermanence" (p. 116) once the back is turned. Cotton growing on the slopes of Mt. Vesuvius, a mountain eloquent in its expression of the fragility of life, reminds Howells that this "cruel plant, so long watered with the tears of slaves, and fed with the blood of men, was now an exile from its native fields, where war was plowing with sword and shot the guilty land, and rooting up the subtlest fibres of the oppression in which cotton had grown king" (p. 95). On the way to the ruins of Herculaneum he passes the New York Coffee House, which if looked into would show some American sailors with "honest, foolish faces flushed with drink" (p. 107).

A telling illustration of the conjunction of New and Old Worlds is found in Howells' account of a walk he takes with a companion upon the Campagna in Rome. He rejoices in the chance the walk gives him of wearying himself "upon that many-memoried ground as freely as if it had been a woods-pasture in Ohio. Nature, where history was so august, was perfectly simple and motherly . . ." (p. 172). Nature, frequently associated with the New World and its innocence (an innocence about to be substantially modified by the consequences of the Civil War), offers Howells a solution to time's obliteration. He voices the solution after viewing the palace of Tiberius: "Nature, the all-forgetting, all-forgiving, that takes the red battlefield into her arms and hides it with blossom and harvest, could not remember his [Tiberius'] iniquity, greater than the multitudinous murder of war" (p. 127). Still, the dilemma remains: nature may forget but man can not.

One senses throughout *Italian Journeys* that the Civil War years have caused Howells to reconsider his attitudes about American innocence and moral superiority. The historic civil excesses of the

Italian city-states, with their bungling attempts to give rational and sustained support to a democratic impulse and their failure to insure more than an occasional moderate tyranny, were lessons from the past which could scarcely be neglected by an idealistic young American witnessing an appalling national slaughter, even if from afar. The ravages of time and the subtle, if disquieting, lessons of history will pose questions for Howells throughout his career as a traveler and writer. To his credit he attempts to use the problem time poses as an organizing principle in *Italian Journeys*.

The decline in spirits of this second travel book, I suspect, can be attributed to Howells' increasing uncertainty about how to come to terms with the past—boyhood and the fresh pastures of Ohio can not forever furnish a refuge from it. The inevitable question must be asked: "What does the past tell me and mean to me as an American?"

Howells, though indirectly, asks the question often. He provides several possible answers, but does not wholly commit himself to a final position. Consequently, any charge that he lacks interest in the past requires some qualification.[42] More accurately, his ideas about it are ambivalent and he has a skeptical view of its uses for modern society. Such a position, arising from moral and utilitarian motives, would help explain some of the assertive statements he makes about the past —statements too often taken as definitive. For example, this statement: "Thank God that the good old times are gone and going! One learns in these aged lands to hate and execrate the past" (*VL*, p. 218). Or this attack on a "dead past—the past which, with all its sensuous beauty and grace, and all its intellectual power, I am not sorry to have dead, and, for the most part, buried" (*IJ*, p. 90).

In fairness one should also consider statements which indicate a different direction. Howells, for example, finds his day at Pompeii a time of "great happiness" (*IJ*, p. 105) because there he sees a more perfect "utterance of the past" (*IJ*, p. 92) than exists anywhere else in the world. In a letter to John Swinton in October of 1863 he reports that though he has concentrated primarily upon "the living human interest" in his Venetian sketches, he could not help imparting some "sentimental and historical relish."[43] Though in 1862 Howells may contend that Italian history is an expression "of an immoral and unjust social order,"[44] he can by the final chapter of *Venetian Life* speak of its subtle influence and of the "pale lustre" which it sheds upon the immediate world.[45]

The attention Howells pays to the "relish" of history has been noted by several of his critics.[46] Certainly his historical method, if it can be called such, would not meet the specifications of a serious historian. When Howells mentions his "grave duty of chronicler,"[47] he obviously enjoys the irony in the statement. On occasion the reader is all too aware of his admitted inability "to write seriously of these ridiculous wicked old shadows."[48] Though Howells does not write seriously and thoroughly about history, he still holds to a few guidelines. Most obviously he tries to do those things not done by such a writer as Bartolomeo Arrighi in his supposedly uninspired account of Mantuan history. Howells avoids lists of events and statistical heaviness, selects details which illustrate character, and seeks the dramatic and anecdotal.[49] By doing so he leaves himself open to charges of oversimplification; one can hardly ignore those times when he appears to sacrifice study of character to humor or facetiousness. Nevertheless, even granting such deficiencies, his early attitudes toward history are instructive, and more complex than they have generally been seen as being.

His attitudes may be roughly stated in the following terms: (1) the present is a more fortunate, if less picturesque, time than the past (*IJ*, p. 63); (2) the experiential, the immediate, and the contemporary are to be preferred to the recorded, the static, and the traditional; (3) the past as it impinges on the present deserves consideration, but a study of it for its own sake is futile; and (4) the reality of the past may frequently be better grasped through sudden insight during travel than through sustained study.

A striking illustration of Howells' preference for the contemporary scene can be seen in his discussion of the excavation of an amphitheater in Verona. After he notices that some small homes nearby have been demolished, he concludes: "To one of the buildings hung a melancholy fire-place left blackened with smoke, and battered with use, but witnessing that it had once been the heart of a home. It was far more touching than any thing in the elder ruin" (*IJ*, p. 305). What has been recently attached to life appeals to him. If a study of the past is to be meaningful, this meaning must come from a search for its present relevance.

When the narrator imaginatively enters a historical scene as an actor or observer (he sometimes does), he evidently does so from a desire to find relevance by re-creating history. He reduces it to an order appropriate to his experience and life. The past, as much as possible, must be experienced and felt. Otherwise it remains sterile and irrelevant. Howells implies as much when discussing "altogether the loveliest room in the world" (*IJ*, p. 315), frescoed by Correggio: "What curious scenes the gayety of this little chamber conjures up, and what a vivid comment it is upon the age and people that produced it! This is one of the things that makes a single hour of travel worth whole years of historic study, and which casts its light upon all future reading" (*IJ*, p. 316). The meaning of the past may suddenly reveal itself in a painting, a ruin, or a church, a revelation which is less possible in systematic study.

Howells also utilizes more usual standards of evaluation when approaching the past. At Pompeii he finds "endless material for study, instruction, and delight" (*IJ*, p. 92). His use of such traditional categories demonstrates once again his dependence upon proven approaches, but perhaps also implies that when the past has some of the character of fiction or *belles lettres* it most appeals to him. When an inner or poetic truth reveals itself through some external object, the relationships between past and present become clearer. If one sees in Howells' approach to antiquity a desire to discover inner truths, and in this sense to be "instructed," then the inclusion of historical material in his travel narratives can be partially explained as an attempt to find a usable past.

The meaning of the past, however, may be very elusive. It may in fact seem unrelated to the present. So far as Howells is concerned, adequate connections between antiquity and contemporary life do not always exist. He expresses doubt about such connections, for example, when he generally discusses the nature of Italian civilization: "The civilization of Italy, as a growth from the earliest pagan times, and only modified by Christianity and the admixture of Northern blood and thought, is yet to be carefully analyzed; and until this analysis is made, discussion of certain features must necessarily be incomplete and unsatisfactory."[50]

Howells' doubts do not, unfortunately, extend as far as his own conclusions about the supposed immorality of past ages. When he discusses some eighteenth-century villas, he feels no regret that life has passed from them. He asks: "How can you feel sympathy for those dull and wicked ghosts of eighteenth-century corruption? There is rottenness enough in the world without digging up old putridity and sentimentalizing on it" (*VL*, p. 389). Such a sweeping indictment as this is not uncommon in either *Venetian Life* or *Italian Journeys*.

The past, divested by time of much of its complexity and vitality, may lead a young writer to the temptation of simple moral solutions. Howells does not always resist this temptation. His voice at times reflects what Nathalia Wright terms "his Puritanically moral view."[51] Though he doubts the adequacy of his treatment of the immorality and promiscuity of the Italians he has observed (*VL*, p. 397), he shows less inclination to doubt his conclusions about the wickedness of the past. His moral certainty probably reflects some defensiveness and insecurity and arises from his own inexperience with a rich and lengthy history. This assurance, however, can be seen as a legitimate reaction against the cruelties of an overly venerated civilization.

In its most positive aspect Howells' moral view of history shows, to use the words of William Jovanovich, a refusal "to accept history if history has the effect of compromising man's respect for himself, of obscuring his ability to distinguish between what is morally conceivable and what is morally inconceivable."[52] In its negative aspect his moral view shows his inexperience and tendency to oversimplify. In future travel writing a more flexible and tolerant Howells will test generalizations about history in the light of accumulated experience and observation.

Howells has as frequently been criticized for his limited treatment of art in his Italian books as for his deficiencies in dealing with history. Even Delmar Gross Cooke, generally enthusiastic about Howells' travel writing, admits that "Some will be disappointed that Howells is so little a technician in the other arts than his own."[53] Clara Marburg Kirk attempts to rectify adverse critical opinions about Howells' response to art. She contends that Howells did possess an adequate aesthetic sense, and that "though he was always a declared amateur in art appreciation, he was throughout his life so fascinated by art that it influenced his theory of writing."[54] Such an influence, however, is not obvious in *Venetian Life* and *Italian Journeys;* there seems little correlation between his literary practice and the methods or techniques noted in the art objects he views. Howells seldom speaks of technical matters relating to the arts. Moreover, his distrust of tradition, of which art frequently serves as a representative, must at least partially qualify his admission near the end of *Venetian Life* of his "sense of the glory and loveliness of Venetian art."[55]

Howells refuses to discuss the beauties and truths of art and architecture on the grounds that language can not suggest such qualities. He excuses himself from a description of a palace by saying: "It is taken for granted that no human being ever yet gained an idea of any building from the most artful description of it."[56] His sense of the inadequacy of language explains some of the reservations he has about Ruskin (though he does depend upon Ruskin's accounts of Venetian art). After he reads Ruskin's description of St. Mark's Church, he begins "to have dreadful doubts of its existence" (*VL*, p. 157). Likewise, the beauties of gothic architecture can at best be thinly sketched "in meagre black and white" (*IJ*, p. 308).

Though Howells usually distrusts authority and the language of art criticism, he ironically enough poses as an authority on occasion; as Firkins notes, "Mr. Howells expressly disclaims the authority which he virtually reclaims from time to time in the decisiveness of some repudiations."[57] The repudiations, when they occur, stem more often from moral criteria than from aesthetic. If he dismisses something for aesthetic reasons, his judgments are quite general. He concludes, for example: "The church of San Moisé is in the highest style of Renaissance art, which is, I believe, the lowest style of any other" (VL, p. 300). He also deplores the luxurious "bad taste" (VL, p. 390) of much Renaissance art. This flaw strikes him as only slightly less opprobrious than the art's lack of spirituality.

In contrast to his blanket assertions are observations and judgments which show him more sensitive and receptive to the value of art. He explicitly mentions that he spent much of his time in Italy viewing art treasures. He feels he is not a green American pretending to be a connoisseur, for when discussing the value of guidebooks he suggests that he has learned something about art on his own. Without guidebooks, he reports, "these painters may be studied and understood, up to a certain point, by one who lives in the atmosphere of their art at Venice, and who, insensibly breathing in its influence, acquires a feeling for it which all the critics in the world could not impart where the works themselves are not to be seen" (VL, p. 156).

His insistence that art must be experienced, that its influence is insensible, and that revelation must come from the works themselves—these, more than an insensitivity to art, explain his reservations. "Special criticisms on art," Howells concludes, "have their small use only in the presence of the works they discuss" (VL, p. 156). In this sense Ruskin has his small use, but his criticism should not be used as a substitute for the experience.

Most criticism has small use, according to Howells, because "critics have no agreement except upon a few loose general principles" (VL, p. 155); consequently, they very little help those wishing to discover truth and beauty in art. Howells' reserve in voicing judgments or opinions about art at this time suggests his belief in certain irreducible dimensions of it. His caution also allows him to remain intellectually honest and to avoid the temptation of aesthetic poses.

Howells himself subscribes to a few loose general principles which he sees as necessary to artistic achievement. Conventionally enough, he frequently implies that good art should be moral art. The doctrinaire tone he assumes, however, when he repudiates "sensual" art makes his judgments of questionable value. The tone frequently suggests more about Howells' notions of sexual propriety than about his interest in aesthetic qualities. He concludes that a monument depicting Grief in the church San Giovanni e Paolo "really represents a drunken woman, whose drapery has fallen, as if in some vile debauch, to her waist, and who broods, with a horrible, heavy stupor and chopfallen vacancy, on something which she supports with her left hand upon her knee" (*VL*, p. 165). A few lines later he compares her to Aphrodite, a "plea-sure-wasted harlot of the sea."

The Italians, Howells admits, share few of his moral principles. And Howells himself grudgingly admires some things which can not be termed morally instructive. One of these is the Chamber of Psyche by Giulio Romano. After seeing it he remarks: "There is scarcely a ray of feeling in Italian art since Raphael's time which suggests Chris-tianity in the artist, or teaches it to the beholder. In confessedly Pagan subjects it was happiest, as in the life of Psyche, in this room; and here it inculcated a gay and spirited license, and an elegant absence of delicacy, which is still observable in Italian life."[58] Even in the pres-ence of such "license" Howells can not deny its imaginative force and the skill evident in the execution. Purely sensuous beauty attracts him, in spite of his moral reservations. He, of course, prefers to be more comfortable when dealing with beauty; one can almost hear an audible sigh of relief when he encounters some specimen of the gothic, a form he considers the highest spiritual expression in man's attempt to create lasting beauty.

Howells believes that serious and moral art finds its best expression in those artists who approach their material realistically. After visiting the German painter, Overbeck, Howells confesses that he discovered "something of the earnestness which animated the elder Christian artists. Overbeck's work is beautiful, but it is unreal, and expresses the sentiment of no time, as the work of the romantic German poets seems without relation to any world men ever lived in" (*IJ*, pp. 170-71).[59] Truthful art must, it seems, ground itself in social realism. Henry James, who much more than Howells finds the time spent among Venice's pictures the best time,[60] also concerns himself with the

issue of realism in Venetian art. He praises Carpaccio and Tintoretto
for being realists and finds it "hard to say which is the more human,
the more various."[61]

Though Howells does not mention the two as realists, his enjoyment of them is indicative. Carpaccio is among the few who give him
"genuine and hearty pleasure" (*VL*, p. 166). Howells finds a painting
of Tintoretto's in the church of Santa Maria dell' Orto expressing "all
his striking imagination in the conception, all his strength in the
drawing and all his lampblack in the faded coloring" (*VL*, p. 213).
Howells, one suspects, sees in the work of these painters a world in
which men have lived, and continue to live. On the other hand, his
rejection of what he sees as the excesses of Renaissance art, particularly the rococo, stems from his conviction that it lacks any relation
to a world that was vital and human.

Thus we see that Howells does not wholly dismiss aesthetic values;
he does find them more congenial to his taste when they can be associated with what is real and moral. Though he makes some sweeping judgments, his conclusions should not be construed as absolute.
He criticizes Ruskin because Ruskin finds necessary connections between aesthetic truth and moral character. Howells rebels when Ruskin attempts to "relate the aesthetic truths you perceive to certain
civil and religious conditions" (*VL*, p. 155), because Howells has discovered that the aesthetic has at best a very limited applicability to
the conduct of real life. When recalling the "intense pleasure" he enjoyed after visiting a few magnificent pictures in Venice, he concludes
by saying: "I could not call the life we led in looking at them an idle
one, even if it had no result in after time. . . ."[62]

Howells' interest in results and his belief that aesthetic "results"
have limited permanence or utility suggest his cultural predicament.
America respects results and teaches her sons to expect, to respect, and
to work toward them. Howells certainly shares these expectations, but
his experience in Europe has had the effects of qualifying, if only
slightly, his conception of the significance of them. In Italy he has
encountered the overwhelming presence of antiquity, and it has come
to have a subtle influence even on one whose concern is most often

with the present scene. The broad perspective of time minimizes the importance of the particular and the practical; it also thwarts his immediate expectations. Frequent modifications of what one expects relaxes expectation and encourages a tendency to accept some things, even aesthetic things, as time gives them.

In many ways Howells' achievement in *Venetian Life* and *Italian Journeys* is an impressive one, even after one hundred years. Both remain very readable, in spite of a degree of ambivalence, inconsistencies in tone, and vacillations in approach. Behind the humorist, the brash critic, the moralist, and the sentimentalist we catch rewarding glimpses of a sensitive and original writer dealing with the manifold problems posed by tradition, convention, history, and art. In seeking answers to these problems he inevitably says much about the central issues of serious travel writing: definition and identification of oneself and one's culture. His inexperience and the uncertainties in his methods preclude completely satisfactory answers to such complex issues.

NOTES

1. Henry James [Review of *Italian Journeys*], *North American Review*, CVI (January 1868), 337.

2. W. D. Howells, *Venetian Life*, 2nd ed. (New York, 1867), p. 15. Subsequent references will be to this edition. When other editions are cited, they will be noted.

3. Joseph A. Dowling cites portions of Conway's review in his unpublished dissertation, "William Dean Howells and his Relationship with the English: A Study of Opinion and Literary Reputation" (Ann Arbor: University Microfilms, 1958), p. 55. An authorized reprint of Dowling's 1957 New York University dissertation.

4. See the unpublished dissertation of George C. Carrington, Jr., "William Dean Howells as a Satirist" (Ann Arbor: University Microfilms, 1961), p. 4. An authorized reprint of a 1959 Ohio State University dissertation.

5. Carrington, p. 18.

6. *Ibid.*, p. 1.

7. Fryckstedt, p. 50.

8. Henry Nash Smith, *Mark Twain: The Development of a Writer* (Cambridge, Mass., 1962), pp. 35-37.

9. W. D. Howells, *Italian Journeys* (New York, 1867), p. 60. Subsequent references will be to this edition. When other editions are cited, they will be noted.

10. James [Review of *Italian Journeys*], p. 339.

11. The correlation between life and drama is interestingly reversed at one point as Howells watches a marionette show. After seeing it he remarks: "Not many passages of real life have affected me as deeply" (*VL*, p. 80). Usually the play of real life has the drama that affects him.

12. James [Review of *Italian Journeys*], p. 338.

13. *Ibid.*

14. Edwin Cady, *The Road to Realism: The Early Years, 1837-1885, of William Dean Howells* (Syracuse, 1956), p. 123.

15. Everett Carter, *Howells and the Age of Realism* (Philadelphia, 1954), p. 45.

16. Howells' disparaging treatment of Byron probably reflects his repugnance for the poet's supposed immorality as much as it does his reservations about his methods. Howells makes Byron a convenient scapegoat for the many abuses and ills done Venice by writers. Moreover, it seems likely that an attack on such a famous and "immoral" figure could hardly help but increase a volume's popularity in America.

17. W. D. Howells, *Venetian Life*, New and Enlarged Ed. (Boston, 1872), pp. 413-14.

18. James [Review of *Italian Journeys*], p. 336.

19. James also finds it convenient to discuss Venice in terms of the drama. In *Italian Hours* (New York, 1959), he observes that "the life of her people and the strangeness of her constitution become a perpetual comedy, or at least a perpetual drama" (p. 28).

20. *Ibid.*, p. 33.

21. *Ibid.*, p. 19.

22. Fryckstedt, pp. 56-57.

23. James, *Italian Hours*, p. 3.

24. Smith, pp. 3-5.

25. Cady, *The Road to Realism*, p. 164.

26. James, *Italian Hours*, p. 34.

27. Fryckstedt, p. 58.

28. Howells' concern for inner truths is seen when he visits Keats' tomb in Rome. He praises the poet for his understanding of "the inner and more fragrant meanings" (*IJ*, p. 168) of external symbols.

29. W. D. Howells, *Italian Journeys*, New and Enlarged Ed. (Boston, 1872), p. 326.

30. *Ibid.*, p. 334.

31. James [Review of *Italian Journeys*], p. 336.

32. *Ibid.*

33. *Italian Journeys*, New and Enlarged Ed., p. 327.

34. *Ibid.*

35. James, in his review of *Italian Journeys*, comments on an "exquisite alternation of natural pathos and humor" (p. 338).

36. Oscar Firkins, *William Dean Howells: A Study* (Cambridge, Mass., 1924), p. 44.

37. Wright, p. 172.

38. James Woodress, *Howells & Italy* (Durham, N.C., 1952), p. 73.

39. W. D. Howells, *Venetian Life*, 2 vols. (Boston, 1891), I, ix.

40. Fryckstedt, for one, finds Howells' treatment of Rome noteworthy more for its omissions than for what is considered (p. 61). Firkins says much the same thing when he reports "a feeling of slimness and poverty growing out of the very rigor of the exclusions that have been made in my behalf" (p. 42). Woodress, who inclines to a more moderate view than the others, nevertheless concludes: "it lacks the unity of the earlier work, and the greater diversity of the subject matter weakens the total impression." Marion Lumpkin Stiles, in an unpublished dissertation, "Travel in the Life and Writings of William Dean Howells" (Austin, Texas, 1946), finds that though the materials and attitudes in *Italian Journeys* are fresh, it still "has become a little thin" (p. 56).

41. Firkins, p. 44.

42. Wright, p. 172.

43. Woodress, p. 52.

44. Fryckstedt, p. 45.

45. *Venetian Life*, New and Enlarged Ed., p. 414.

46. Woodress speaks of "engaging bits of history" (p. 62) in the travel books. Stiles finds "Ducal Mantua" "in Howells' best style, which made all history simple and interesting" (p. 48). Firkins concludes: "Toward history his attitude is debonair" (p. 48).

47. *Italian Journeys*, New and Enlarged Ed., p. 381.

48. *Ibid.*, p. 347.

49. *Ibid.*, p. 327.

50. *Ibid.*, p. 377.

51. Wright, p. 171.

52. William Jovanovich, "The Misuses of the Past," *Saturday Review* (April 2, 1966), p. 23.

53. Delmar G. Cooke, *William Dean Howells: A Critical Study* (New York, 1922), p. 137. Cooke shares a view with Firkins in being grateful that Howells refrains from reporting what has too often been reported. Firkins as well praises Howells for being humanely brief in his descriptions of architecture (p. 47).

Fryckstedt and Wright are less certain of the merit of so slight a consideration of so important a subject. They both conclude that he has slight aesthetic sensibility.

54. Kirk, *Howells and Art*, p. 31.
55. *Venetian Life*, New and Enlarged Ed., p. 431.
56. *Italian Journeys*, New and Enlarged Ed., p. 360.
57. Firkins, p. 47.
58. *Italian Journeys*, New and Enlarged Ed., p. 378.
59. Howells, with characteristic ambivalence, admits to having an illogical pleasure in looking at Overbeck's "subjective" drawings (*IJ*, p. 170).
60. James, *Italian Hours*, p. 17.
61. *Ibid.*, p. 27.
62. *Venetian Life*, New and Enlarged Ed., p. 432.

3

THE LESSONS AND LIMITATIONS
OF ALTRUISM

A second trip to Italy in 1882, lasting nearly a year, furnished Howells with material for two new travel books, *Tuscan Cities* (1886) and *A Little Swiss Sojourn* (1892).[1] His sojourn in Switzerland pleased him, but, as Woodress notes, he found Italy "older and dingier" after twenty years,[2] and ironically enough, Howells' disillusionment with Italy prompted a book superior in most respects to *Italian Journeys*. Firkins suggests the tenor of critical estimates about Howells' travel account of Switzerland when he curtly dismisses it as "one of those monographs to which time is hardly favorable."[3]

Howells treatment of the Swiss lacks the freshness, the color, and the wit evident in his other travel books. At his best when he writes of St. Bonivard, whom he obviously admires for his skepticism and untrammeled spirit,[4] he demonstrates less obvious enthusiasm for the contemporary Swiss and their country. Italy, by virtue of its colorful inhabitants, long history, and art treasures, elicits a more imaginative and critical response from him. The material for which he usually demonstrates an aptitude he mentions only in passing; the dominance of the Swiss women and the surliness of the men (p. 37), for example, receive little notice. He feels that the Swiss have many characteristics

in common with New Englanders (p. 37), but he does not actively explore the implications arising from the parallels. The same holds true
when he notes the similarities in American and Swiss political institutions (pp. 74-75).

Tuscan Cities has received more attention than *A Little Swiss Sojourn;* however, it has hardly elicited the favorable critical response
accorded the two earlier Italian travel books. Edwin Cady rightly suggests that Howells found his "refresher course" in European culture
a disappointment: "The old, golden glamor of Italy was gone. He
could find grace and aesthetic solace in Florence; but amid the squalor
and hopelessness of the people—and even in the face of the Italian
past with its awful histories of bloodshed and betrayal—he experienced
dismay and disillusion, as much with his younger self as with Italy.
At any rate, Henry James' question as to whether an American novelist
did not have to live abroad and deal with international society, a question which had remained in abeyance with Howells during his years
of magazine service, was answered. America was his place."[5]

A sense of disillusionment and a sharper critical tone are notable
features of *Tuscan Cities;* however, just as apparent are technical
problems, equal in magnitude, if different in kind from those evident
in his earlier books. Because *Tuscan Cities* was written at the time of
such fine fiction as *A Modern Instance* (1882), *The Rise of Silas Lapham* (1885), and *Indian Summer* (1886), its weaknesses suggest that it
is an important failure. The discrepancy between the attempt and the
achievement signals a crucial stage in Howells' development as a
travel writer—as does the disparity between his sensitivity and the
techniques he employs for revealing that sensitivity. One feels indeed
that *Tuscan Cities* reflects Howells' uneasy discovery that he can not
be a realist in fiction and something else in other forms of literature.
He has attempted, perhaps because of this uneasiness, to make the
travel book something more than it can comfortably be. *Tuscan Cities*
must prove explicitly theses about altruism, democracy, the uses of
art, and the meaning of the past. Because it is under such obligations,
it shows signs of strain.

The seriousness of the book seems far from Howells' original intentions for it, if we may judge by the readiness with which he approached the writing of some "semi-historical sketches" in the manner of the long chapter on Ducal Mantua in *Italian Journeys*.[6] He proposed to give the reader "anecdote and adventure" from history rather than a thorough treatment of it.[7] Though faithful to his declared purpose, he apparently came to recognize that he could no longer write so easily about the actualities of a foreign land, either present or past.

Some of the issues evident in his earlier books again prove troublesome. A central issue, to which most technical considerations are referable, is the applicability of the methods of fictional realism to the travel book. Howells' advocacy of the practices of realism in fiction prompts one to question whether his belief has not led to changes in his conception of the methods proper to travel writing. A second major issue has to do with the past and the uses of history. The past, with which he earlier established an uneasy truce, impinges more forcibly on the present than ever—and seems no less enigmatic. The third issue concerns art. Mostly cured of out-of-hand repudiations of works of art, Howells still speaks reluctantly about art, yet, the attention paid the possible relationships between the arts and the duties of artists to society reveals a more than casual concern. The numerous illustrations by Joseph Pennell and others, which fill the pages of the volume, also point to his concern for possible connections between artistic media.

An adequate exploration of these three broad areas in turn hinges on understanding the implications of several of Howells' attitudes about travel. Howells sees the travel book as a vehicle for recording reexperienced history; he strongly urges a commitment to humanitarian ideals; and he feels that Italy, above all countries, is the home of human nature for the traveler. Consideration of these attitudes leads to fuller conclusions about the art of travel writing and the necessities of conscience.

Early in *Tuscan Cities* Howells takes care to justify the historical bent of his work. When in the study at home, he says, "one may read history, but one can realize it, as if it were personally experienced, only on the spot where it was lived. This seems to me the prime use of travel; and to create the reader a partner in the enterprise and a sharer in its realization seems the sole excuse for books of travel, now when modern facilities have abolished hardship and danger and adventure and nothing is more likely to happen to one in Florence than in Fitchburg."[8]

Howells attempts to create a prose mode flexible enough either to accommodate a general historical narrative or to convey the personal significance of fiction or drama; he will also imbue history, as much as possible, with immediate relevance. He ironically argues that creating a realization of the past is the "sole excuse" for travel books. His earlier books certainly did not insist on such a necessity. Though Howells emphasizes the realization of history, other kinds of realizations do more to create the charm and vitality of the account than do the historical ones.

Woodress praises Howells for his ability to write of history "in a manner which a professional historian might envy."[9] I see fewer positive virtues in travel-book history. In 1875, when Howells appreciatively reviewed James' *Transatlantic Sketches,* he noted that the sketches were unusual in that they offered no history to the reader;[10] but he nowhere implied that they suffer for the absence. It is unlikely that Howells would propose a single criterion (the "sole excuse") for travel writing in light of his awareness of James' approach. Nor does his experience as a reviewer of travel books suggest only one standard. At any rate, Howells does demonstrate a greater concern for history than he did in the earlier Italian books.

In *Tuscan Cities* Howells' concern for making the reader a sharer in the realizations of history often is less important than his interest in the evolution of democracy in Italy.[11] His frequent reference to democracy and tyranny implies a marked commitment to democratic ideals and forms, and his search through Italian history for its moments of altruism also suggests a moral and didactic intention. Unfortunately, such a search has negative implications since the weighty proofs about the follies and oppressions of the past have the effect of raising serious questions about the possibility of avoiding them.

Though Howells feels that the travel book can treat history, he has reservations about the use of history in fiction. When walking up the Via de Bardi in Florence, "for the sake of Romola, whose history begins there" (p. 64), he feels that George Eliot burdens "her drama and dialogue with too much history" (p. 65). Certainly in *Indian Summer* history plays only a minor part. By 1900, as Carter observes, Howells still believed that most writers could not adequately re-create the past. Howells suggests that " 'it is hard to get nature to take part in one's little effects when it is an affair of contemporary life; if it is an affair of life in the past her co-operation is still more reluctant.' "[12]

Nature hesitates to cooperate in re-creating the past insofar as her laws treating perspective inevitably create "a false impression" (p. 42). Though the realization of the past may be somewhat different from its re-creation, the issue of perspective seems relevant to both. The declining enthusiasm with which Howells looks at historical events in *Tuscan Cities* suggests that the attempt to realize history has not proved a profitable exercise.

To help the reader realize the past, Howells frequently dramatizes it. Yet when he asks his reader—"Is it perhaps all a good deal too much like a stage-play? Or is it that stage-plays are too much like facts of this sort?" (p. 74)—one is tempted to accept, with few reservations, the first proposition. Of the second the reader might remark that his guide, after all, has selected the facts and sacrificed thoroughness to interest. The generalizations arising from the dramatic scenes strongly suggest the democratic bias of the volume. They, however, are less the issue than the ease with which they are summoned. The discrepancy between the serious intent of the generalizations and the lightness of the method leading to them stands as the primary problem of the volume.

Howells seems to sense a conflict between his ideas and his method when he states, near the end of the chapter on Florence, that he had "an intention of studying Florence more seriously than anything here represents" (p. 107). Though he originally intended to concern himself largely with the past, by the end of his account of Florence he confesses that present Florence attracts him much more: "my heart still warms to the famous town, not because of that past which, however heroic and aspiring, was so wrong-headed and bloody and pitiless, but because of the present, safe, free, kindly, full of possibilities of prosperity and fraternity, like that of Boston and Denver" (p. 122).

Howells' attitude about the past is still ambivalent, a characteristic observable when he apostrophizes at one point: "Poor, splendid, stupid, glorious past!" (p. 155).[13] He may, when pursuing the past, "surprise himself in the possession of a genuine emotion" (p. 18), but he may just as often complain of his "unhappy acquaintance" with it (p. 69) or ironically assert his kinship with its more serious chroniclers (p. 197). While on the one hand he seeks to transmit a realization to his reader, on the other he concedes that he never manages to lose himself in the associations with the past.

Though he tries to give the reader the feeling of the "sweet confusion of travel in . . . old lands" (p. 204), one senses that the confusion is not always so sweet. Lacking a history, the American becomes acutely conscious of one which in many ways seems insubstantial to him. Raw and unhistoried as he is, he inevitably has a strong sense of the present and of fluid existence. Howells, though he attempts to establish rapport with Italy, admits the difficulty of doing so in a letter to Thomas Sergeant Perry. In America, he adds, "we have the country of the present and the future."[14] Even if Howells' statement is a little ironic, which it may be, his assertion points as accurately as anything to the problem he faces in writing of the past when his sympathies lie so much with the present and the hope of the future; an inescapable tension and ambivalence result.

Howells' semi-history also suffers, in a sense, from its burden of idealism—which is not to suggest that the idealism is necessarily misplaced. His deepened social conscience, which prompts a desire for enlightened democratic government, has encouraged in him a didactic view of history. When discussing the strange hold Savonarola has upon men's minds, he concludes: "all history, like each little individual experience, enforces nothing but this lesson of altruism; and it is because the memory which consecrates the church of San Marco teaches it in supreme degree that one stands before it with a swelling heart" (pp. 59-60).

Howells' search for evidences of altruism leads him to pay particular attention to those who have either flagrantly denied the altruistic
impulse or who have affirmed it by exercising a "genius for humanity"; Howells terms this genius "about the only kind of genius which
is entitled to reverence in this world" (p. 91). During his travels
through the past he discovers numerous tyrants, but meets few good
men who have had this genius. These few, in governing wisely or
acting justly, command more respect that most sculptors, novelists,
and poets, who have merely depicted the beautiful and the pleasurable.

Thus Howells praises, in Siena, Bandini and Socinus, the first as
"the inventor of Free Trade in commerce," and the second as "the
inventor of Free Thought in religion" (p. 134). In "pitiless" Pisa, on
the other hand, he wonders if some of the artists might be mocking
the religion for which they paint. In criticizing some supposedly "atro-
cious" work of Orgagna, he states: "I for one will not pretend to have
revered those works of art, or to have felt anything but loathing in
their presence. If I am told that I ought at least to respect the faith
with which the painter wrought, I say that faith was not respectable"
(p. 211). Clara Kirk suggests that by the time of *Criticism and Fiction*
(1891), "a belief in the social obligation of art had . . . become a
fundamental part of his philosophy";[15] in *Tuscan Cities* this belief
is already apparent.

As well as voicing his belief in the duties of art and the responsibilities of artists, Howells advocates the dignity of all work (p. 113). He
also recognizes the necessity for freedom, "a means to peace" (p. 74),
and praises fraternal and egalitarian impulses whenever they appear.
In an "Editor's Study," written a year after the publication of his
travel volume, he nearly offers in eloquent summary those ideas oc-
curring in *Tuscan Cities* as scattered reflections. Democracy in literature, he states, "wishes to know and to tell the truth, confident that
consolation and delight are there; it does not care to paint the marvelous and impossible for the vulgar many, or to sentimentalize and falsify
the actual for the vulgar few. Men are more like than unlike one
another; let us make them know one another better, that they may
be all humbled and strengthened with a sense of their fraternity.

Neither arts, nor letters, nor sciences, except as they somehow, clearly or obscurely, tend to make the race better and kinder, are to be regarded as serious interests; they are idle, and they cannot do this except from and through the truth."[16] After reading *Tuscan Cities* one can not help feeling that his Italian experience has been instrumental, to some degree, in shaping these beliefs.

Howells' belief that literature has a duty to help ameliorate social conditions stems, at least in *Tuscan Cities,* from his recognition of self-satisfying and self-destructive impulses in man. Just before going to Europe he reviewed J. B. Harrison's *Certain Dangerous Tendencies in American Life,* and what he says of Harrison's work anticipates what he will say in *Tuscan Cities.* Harrison has been mistakenly called pessimistic, Howells maintains. Harrison is not pessimistic in recognizing "needlessly deplorable conditions" nor in suggesting that men are essentially the same.[17] Nor is Harrison pessimistic in finding in man "faults of character and mind not radical but well nigh inveterate."[18] Howells discovers striking evidence of more radical faults in man. Savagery, he observes, "lurks so near the surface in every man that a constant watch must be kept upon the passions and impulses, or he leaps out in his war-paint, and the poor integument of civilization that held him is flung aside like a useless garment" (p. 43). Italy, "above all lands the home of human nature" (p. 96), provides Howells some striking evidence of irrationality and disruptions of civil life. Presumably the conclusions he draws about the human condition in Italy have wide applicability.

Thus it is, when the Florentines of a cruel past strike Howells as absurd and encourage him "to a certain mood of triviality" (p. 42), they tempt him hardly more than any other citizenry might. One may be led to a trivial mood by the unaugust events of history, but an equal danger exists that one's conscience may be confounded (p. 52). The cruelty and depravity of the famous Lorenzo of the Medicis may meet with almost unqualified success; Howells wryly notes that poetic justice and God's justice are very different things. The success of those like Lorenzo leads him to question whether evil may sometimes be a more powerful influence in the universe than good (p. 74).[19] Certainly much historical evidence points to this possibility; this evidence, in turn, has the effect of making any altruistic action precious.

No man's motives, however, can be accepted without question. During a description of a drive with Joseph Pennell through the countryside near Lucca, Howells and Pennell see human nature in action: "From the grass, the larks were quivering up to the perfect heaven, and the sympathy of Man with the tender and lovely mood of Nature was expressed in the presence of the hunters with their dogs, who were exploring the herbage in quest of something to kill" (pp. 221-22). Howells then concludes: "Perhaps I do man injustice. Perhaps the rapture of the blameless *littérateur* and artist, who drove along crying out over the exquisite beauty of the scene, was more justly representative of our poor race" (p. 222). Howells speaks ironically of his and Pennell's blamelessness and knows that their rapture is less representative than man's inclination "to kill."

His composite view of "our poor race," past or present, is hardly cheerful. Though the race seems capable of moments of rationality and occasional flashes of humanitarian genius, it has more often been characterized by the reverse. Howells concludes that even American democracy, which should insure the practice and affirm the principle of brotherhood, appears much better in theory than in practice (p. 91). Nevertheless, the democratic system gives man a better chance than he might otherwise have, particularly in the absence of divine guidance. For, as Howells observes, "few of us are ever sufficiently in the divine confidence to be able to say just why this or that thing happens, and we are constantly growing more modest about assuming to know" (p. 45).

In a democracy, where man is allowed to find his own answers, he has great responsibility toward his fellows; he must, Howells implies, guarantee dignity and insure peace to preserve civilization. In attempting to perform so overwhelming a task, the individual will very likely fail, as Savonarola failed, but such failure paradoxically contributes to collective success. This idea, strongly implied in *Tuscan Cities,* is stated in *Indian Summer* by Mr. Waters as he and Colville discuss the meaning of Savonarola's failure: " 'Men fail, but man succeeds. I don't know what it all means, or any part of it; but I have had moods in which it seemed as if the whole mystery were about to flash upon me.' "[20]

Howells' desire to discover the meaning of the mystery and his awareness of the difficulty of doing so are central concerns in the travel book. His sense of the mystery leads him to subscribe to democratic ideals. His advocacy of these ideals, in turn, arises from his awareness of man's fallibilities—not from an easy optimism or a belief in individual perfectibility. The tension existing between the idealist's desire for universal brotherhood and the realist's concern for the actualities of existence makes *Tuscan Cities* a social document which repays careful study.

When compared to his earlier travel accounts, it reveals a finer critical sense, an increased social sensitivity, and a more serious concern for the issues of man's existence. Though Howells sees deep shadows on the human landscape, and speaks of somber conditions, his writing is affirmative, and perhaps a modest claim for recognition might be made on this account. Robert Penn Warren suggests: "the literature that is most truly and profoundly critical is always the most profoundly affirmative."[21] If *Tuscan Cities* is not profoundly critical, it at least leans in that direction. The prevailing critical mood prompted Firkins to conclude, accurately enough, that the volume contains only "fitful and elusive sunshine."[22]

The dangers of turning scattered commentary into a consistent program are real enough, and perhaps I have not altogether escaped those dangers. Yet it can not be disputed that the good humor, the iconoclasm, the extravagance, and the brash assurances of his earlier work have yielded to more serious matters. The life Howells sees in Italy, as a traveler through past and present, has had the effect of raising significant political, ideological, and moral questions. No wonder then that Howells complains that his fancy is overworked (p. 178); the demands of truth have become more rigorous than they were in the Italy of his youth, and fancy appears uncertain of her station and function amid such serious material. Fancy's fatigue is symptomatic of how large concerns determine the character and appropriateness of the techniques Howells uses. By examining these techniques, one learns much about the issue of realistic practice in the travel book.

Tuscan Cities surpasses the two early books in consistency of tone and handling of point of view. Howells' "general," or omniscient, voice, conditioned by his years as editor and reviewer for the *Atlantic*, has become surer, less facetious, and less condescending. He generalizes frequently, but not absolutely, and usually bases his generalizations on observation or authority. His familiar or narrative voice, on the other hand, does not become cloyed with rhapsodic or sentimental language. He still finds the sentimentalist abounding in Italy (p. 14), but he is no longer one. In general he speaks in a more serious voice. The light irony which pleased his earlier readers has become sharper and darker. He still speaks fancifully, but his fancy too often strains for an effect—a fact which he seems to recognize. And though he is more aware of the issue of point of view, he has problems with it.

A new and noticeable feature in *Tuscan Cities* is the author's assumption of a known audience. Contrary to his usual practice in fiction, Howells from time to time confides in his reader. He attempts to make his reader a partner, probably to promote the illusion of participation. He also utilizes other devices to let his reader know how conscientious he is as a guide, how aware of his charge's welfare. He confesses that he writes in Boston rather than in Siena; he unashamedly admits that he relies on his notebook to refresh his memory (p. 176). At another time he playfully refers to *Venetian Life* as a "classic" (p. 92), and at yet another alludes obliquely to a visit he and his wife made to Pistoia nearly twenty years before (p. 237). Generally his allusions and addresses to the reader are casual; they do, however, suggest an awareness of his reputation as a writer and demonstrate a heightened consciousness of his motives.

He treats his audience less than gently. He criticizes his reader, and himself, often enough to create an expectancy for abuse. For example, he ironically criticizes the reader's snobbishness when discussing the popular amusements in Florence. His more polite readers, whom he always accounts "extremely well-behaved and well-dressed persons" (p. 103), he excludes from these amusements; the less elegantly clothed Florentines find these highly entertaining fare. Perhaps impatient with such standard accounts as readers usually get, Howells on occasion insists that the reader must furnish his own facts, impressions (p. 208), or scenic prospects (p. 251).

Faced with a steadily growing number of such imperatives, an increasingly wary reader hardly knows what to make of such a familiar address as this: "Do you remember, beloved brethren and sisters of Florentine sojourn, the little windows beside the grand portals of the palaces?" (p. 116). Is Howells here affirming a sentimental kinship with Florentine sojourners, ridiculing the intrusive, familiar voice he finds so distasteful in much fiction, or is he merely being ironically irreverent toward his readers? All three alternatives appear defensible, and the address has the merit of conscious ambiguity.

If the address suggests some sense of impatience, and perhaps ambivalence, about his methods, material, and audience, it has a more positive aspect in pointing to an issue of realism. I suspect that Howells, in capitalizing on his reputation as a defender of realistic fiction, quite consciously uses such devices as the confidential aside or the direct and intimate address for critical purposes. Would not those readers already in realism's camp be amused to find one of their champions using, with irony, the very methods he normally criticizes? To the later reader of *Tuscan Cities,* however, for whom the din of battle over realistic fiction has considerably diminished, the familiar address probably comes as something of a surprise; it may suggest an evasion of descriptive or critical responsibility more than an ironic perspective.

Much more disquieting than the presence of an intrusive authorial voice is the narrator's practice of making himself a character in dramatic scenes of the past. In speaking of this approach to history Howells observes: "One of the advantages of this method is that you have your historical personages in a sort of picturesque contemporaneity with one another and with yourself, and you imbue them with all the sensibilities of our own time. Perhaps this is not an advantage but it shows what may be done by the imaginative faculty; and if we do not judge men by ourselves, how are we to judge them at all?" (p. 18). But, as Marion Stiles observes, Howells' readers are not apt to be enthusiastic about such a method.[23] I do not dispute the accuracy of Howells' final statement, but a preceding statement, about judging in terms of present sensibilities, strikes me as one-sided. Characters from the past will inevitably be invested with present sensibilities, but perhaps an author has a responsibility to discover and to delineate, as well as he can, past sensibilities, in order better to understand and judge himself and his fellows.

Howells feels that dramatizing history effectively creates interest, and he assumes a carefree manner when upon the historical stage. When viewing a past seige of Florence—and at the same time listening to a recitation of a Browning poem—his "embattled fancy" wings over the battleground, "sallying, repulsing, defeating, succumbing" (p. 67). The author admits fatigue after such strenuous activity. The reader, I suspect, feels equally tired.

The same reader, if he hesitates to listen to a talking city, will hardly be receptive when Howells and Pisa, old friends, talk in melancholy tones. Pisa, made an accomplice to a pun on *The Century* magazine, sadly confesses: " 'I remember no century, since the fifteenth, when—I—died' " (p. 201). Howells and Pennell turn away from the grieving city "with our hearts in our throat" (p. 201). Though the exchange could possibly be construed as consciously melodramatic and absurd, it seems contrived, and suggests facetiousness more than anything else. Howells' fancy creates interest at the expense of probability, and the question arises whether, after all, the reality of the past should be sacrificed so thoroughly to the exercise of the imaginative faculty.

When Howells attempts more serious dramatic encounters, he does not have unqualified success. Consider, for example, the narrator's role during this re-creation of an attempted assassination of the infamous Lorenzo de Medici in the cathedral:

> Lorenzo's sword is out and making desperate play for his life; his friends close about him, and while the sacred vessels are tumbled from the altar and trampled under foot in the mellay [sic], and the cathedral rings with yells and shrieks and curses and the clash of weapons, they have hurried him into the sacristy

and barred the doors, against which we shall beat ourselves in vain. Fury! Infamy! Malediction! Pick yourself up, Francesco Pazzi, and get home as you may! There is no mounting to horse and crying liberty through the streets for you! All is over! The wretched populace, the servile signory, side with the Medici; in a few hours the Archbishop of Pisa is swinging by the neck from a window of the Palazzo Vecchio, and while he is yet alive you are dragged, bleeding and naked, from your bed through the streets and hung beside him so close that in his dying agony he sets his teeth in your breast with a convulsive frenzy that leaves you fast in the death-clutch of his jaws till they cut the rope and you ruin [sic] hideously down to the pavement below (pp. 54-55).

The passage is vivid and vigorous—an effect created in part by the spectacular nature of the details, but also by the skilful use of the present tense, the sharp imperative statements, and the rapid movement of the prose.

The narrator, however, takes upon himself some unusual tasks. He gives stage directions at the same time he and the reader must serve as observers and actors; he additionally describes, judges, and gives advice. When he commands Francesco Pazzi home and then tells the victim the graphic details of his death as he dies, he seems in too many places at once. Of course, when the narrator is only a "frivolous tourist" (p. 68) and can become a Florentine by the merest exercise of the imagination, few things are impossible; one can be both the gentlest of tourists and the most ferocious of combatants, "in the presence of occasions sufficiently remote" (p. 70).

Howells does suggest that he recites the "grisly details" of the attempted assassination in order to give the reader a feel for Florence's past (p. 55). The voice he uses, however, is not altogether convincing, and such details frequently suggest as much about the author's methods as they do about historical Florence; one has much more feeling for the figures of the present than for the illustrious ones from the past. The commonplace and trivial of average and contemporaneous experience, which he renders so finely, are precisely those things missing during the author's journeys into the past. Consequently, the frequent moments when he returns to the present, finds a drying wash in Dante's old neighborhood (p. 31) or shivers in the icy, dim room of the Villa Careggi, where Lorenzo perished centuries before (p. 56), are the best moments.

When Howells presents contemporary figures his effects resemble those in his novels. Freed from a bondage of generalized action, from a succession of irreversible facts, and from the necessity of being a vigorous participant in the past, he writes more calmly and speaks with a more consistent voice. Seemingly less self-conscious, he does not need to loose a straining fancy. One could ask for nothing finer than this description of a young Sienese woman: "a young lady, doubtless of the ancient family to which the palace belonged, came out upon the terrace from the first floor with an elderly companion, and loitering listlessly there a moment, descended the steps into the garden to a stone basin where some serving-women were washing. Her hair was ashen blond; she was slimly cased in black, and as she slowly walked, she pulled forward the skirt a little with one hand, while she drew together with the other a light shawl, falling from the top of her head, round her throat; her companion followed at a little distance; on the terrace lingered a large white Persian cat, looking after them" (p. 147). The woman lingers upon the page for only a moment, but she, more than any figure of the past, is "realized"—and without dramatic apparatus. The simplicity of the scene, the objective presentation, the relaxed tone, and the sense of grace Howells manages to suggest in the character's movement and dress create a charming effect.

Howells' shortcoming as an historian lies in his inability to find in the past this suggestive detail which speaks so ably for itself and contributes so effectively to characterization. As a consequence he attempts to vivify his historical figures through the energy of his narrator's speech and the strenuous movements of the narrator and other actors upon the historical stage; he also tries to impart as much vitality as possible by establishing and maintaining a rapid narrative pace.

Though Howells' idea of history is anthropocentric (his method implies that individual men give it direction and relevance rather than merely reflecting it), those men from the past who appear upon his pages nevertheless lack the trappings of concrete existence; they remain remote in spite of the attempt to make them alive and contemporary. Lorenzo and Savonarola may well have been involved in a "profound drama" (p. 57) of liberty and tyranny, but they have more the nature of abstractions or shadows than the concrete feel of mortality. Howells' strength in *Tuscan Cities,* as Delmar Cooke concludes, is in deftly "catching the fleeting bit of life or sense, so pregnant and so illusive."[24]

The techniques Howells uses to render character differ considerably from some he professes to admire in other histories of Florence. He praises the histories for "the circumstantial minuteness with which they are told, and their report has an air of simple truth very different from the literary facetiousness which one is tempted to in following them. After six centuries the passions are as living, the characters as distinct, as if the thing happened yesterday. Each of the persons stands out a very man or woman, in that clear, strong light of the early day which they move through" (p. 28). That Howells shows an interest in the living passions, finds the past bathed in such bright light, and admires an air of simple truth is surprising—especially since in his fiction he concerns himself with complexity of motive and character interaction, in his travel books usually associates the past with twilight (p. 195), and feels that "living passions" too often find their way into sentimental or melodramatic accounts.[25]

The simplicity he praises creates problems for him; in attempting to impart to his characters a similar simplicity, he inclines to be facetious. Moreover, his characters illustrate or explain ideas and moral beliefs more than they stand for themselves. They suffer from being nudged too often in the direction of an explicit thesis. Unlike their fellows in the novel, they do not have their lives modified by circumstance, qualified by behavior and social conditions, or tested pragmatically by action and experience.

A more positive manifestation of simplicity can be observed in Howells' prose, if it is contrasted to earlier samples. He has come to distrust the sentimental and the rhetorical, as he suggests when he calls attention to a passage he has just written: "It is not my habit to write such fine rhetoric as this [about Siena], the reader will bear me witness" (p. 126). Though he avoids such rhetoric, he playfully, and ironically, allows a fellow writer the practice of it. After quoting the writer's eulogy of the Sienese character, Howells casually concludes that save for a reference to Dante, he might have thought he was reading an account praising the perfections of the American character (p. 129).

A concern for the "daily bread of common speech," mentioned in Howells' 1875 review of James' European travel sketches, appears in *Tuscan Cities*. He, for example, praises the simplicity and eloquence with which Michelangelo expresses the loss of liberty. The artist's words strike him as "nobly simple, and of a colloquial and natural pitch to which their author seldom condescended in sculpture" (p. 76). Because Howells believes that ornament and affectation impede accurate representation, in language as well as in art, it seems fitting that he should praise a seventeenth-century writer, Richard Lassels. Lassels writes of aesthetic matters with "a beautiful succinctness, a tranquil brevity" (p. 212).

If we turn to consider Howells' own prose, we can justifiably say that it is economical, clear, and finely modulated. A representative example is the following description of a cloister in Florence: "I remember particularly an evening effect in the cloister of Santa Annunziata, when the belfry in the corner, lifted aloft on its tower, showed with its pendulous bells like a great, graceful flower against the dome of the church behind it. The quiet of the place was almost sensible; the pale light, suffused with rose, had a delicate clearness; there was a little agreeable thrill of cold in the air; there could not have been a more refined moment's pleasure offered to a sympathetic tourist loitering slowly homeward to his hotel and its *table d' hôte;* and why we cannot have old cloisters in America, where we are getting everything that money can buy, is a question that must remain to vex us" (p. 97). The long initial sentence suggests, in its movement, an upward and extended gaze. Those following, in their brevity, simplicity, and unobtrusive parallel phrasing, are appropriate to the silence, the clearness, the thrill of cold. The lines describing the loitering tourist suggest that scant exertion through long vowel sounds. The scene concludes in the wry observation about America's answer to tranquillity. The ironic look the speaker directs at his "refinement" serves to heighten, even more, the tension between the aesthetic and the practical and to suggest the complexity of the authorial perspective.

The self-conscious rhetoric found occasionally in *Venetian Life* and *Italian Journeys* has vanished. The flow of feeling has been checked and cleansed of its imperfections by a maturer critical perspective and a heightened skepticism.[26] Though Howells does not record the minutest of detail nor graphically delineate a scene, he does fashion a subtly suggestive prose. His sentences move gracefully and naturally, often complementing content by rhythms. His style, more than formerly, finely expresses his travel experience and the perceptions arising from it.

One suggestive, if conclusive, sidelight to the issue of realism in the travel book stems from Howells' interest in the photograph as a surface upon which reality may be recorded. When he typically enough declines to describe the cathedral in Siena, he suggests to his readers: "Get photographs, get prints, dear reader, or go see for yourself!" (p. 173). Since *Tuscan Cities* is filled with Pennell's illustrations, what Howells requests of the reader is odd. Evidently he liked Pennell's work, for in an "Editor's Study" of 1886 he suggests that in *Tuscan Cities* "Mr. Pennell has done some of his best work, which is always gay, bright, honest, and expressive of the joy of doing."[27] Elsewhere Howells appears less enthusiastic about photographs; at one point he concludes about them: "The photographs do well enough in suggestion for such as have not seen the church, but these will never have the full sense of it which only long looking and coming again and again can impart" (p. 167). Though nearly every place and scene in Italy has been so much photographed that "few can have any surprise left in them" (p. 97), the eye can nevertheless find a "full sense" impossible in a photograph. Howells apparently sees the photograph as having limited realistic function, yet he will again consider the possible relationships between photography and realism in his later travel books, particularly in *London Films*.

Howells' interest in the photograph's ability to record reality indicates a general tendency in this travel book: he frequently points his observations, techniques or allusions toward the issues of realistic writing. Such techniques as point of view, as we have seen, often stand in ironic contrast to the author's usual practice in fiction. In one way or another Howells touches upon such things as appropriateness of material, fidelity in representation, style and language, the inconclusiveness of experience, and methods of characterization.

Where the matter at hand is characterization, for example, Howells shows some characters at Doney's, a famous cafe in Florence, to illustrate his point. He passes over them quickly. Longer investigation, he concludes, "might even have impaired their value in the picture of a conscientious artist who can now leave them, without a qualm, to be imagined as rich and noble as the reader likes" (p. 23). This statement, of course, implicitly criticizes the writers and readers of fiction who prefer "noble" characters. But it also suggests that the serious artist knows that character must be created rather than assumed. He knows, too, that inconclusiveness in characterization can be a virtue; one who requires absolute knowledge of character demands more than real life can afford him.

The undercurrent of critical suggestion found throughout *Tuscan Cities* does more than demonstrate Howells' concern about the issues of realism; it also shows his sensitivity to his own motives and intentions. During the course of the book, he often enough questions his own sincerity (as well as the lack of it in the artists whose work he views) to convince his reader that a search for intention may not be profitable. However, he does explicitly state his structural intentions toward the end of "A Florentine Mosaic." In doing so he consciously does something he would not do as a writer of fiction. He does, however, express reservations about such intentions as he has— and invites the reader to share in his reservation about the appropriateness of the metaphor which expresses the structural intent:

Few of my readers, I hope, have failed to feel the likeness of these broken and ineffectual sketches to the pictures in stone which glare at you from the windows of the mosaicists on the Lungarno and in the Via Borgognissante; the wonder of them is greater than the pleasure. I have myself had the fancy, in my work, of a number of small views and figures of mosaic, set in a slab of black marble for a table-top, or—if the reader does not like me to be so ambitious—a paper-weight; and now I am tempted to form a border to this *capo d' opera,* bizarre and irregular, such as I have sometimes seen composed of bits of *pietra viva* left over from a larger work. They are mere fragments of color, scraps and shreds of Florence, which I find still gleaming more or less dimly in my note-books, and I have no notion of making any ordered arrangement. (pp. 115-16)

Howells chooses a happy metaphor suggesting as it does both the limitations of the art and the possibilities for order. He makes use of sharp contrasts and deftly fits bits and fragments into a larger pattern. Interested more in the bright color of character and scene than in continuity of experience or thoroughness of investigation, he still adds to the value of his "small views and figures" by setting them against the serious background of his skepticism and social concerns.

Perhaps I make more of the metaphor than Howells would wish. Yet, I suspect the reservations he expresses about the "broken and ineffectual sketches" should not be accepted as definitive. I find the sketches quite carefully patterned. A hint of the care expended is observable in the parallelism in the opening and closing of the essay. It begins with an account of Howells' arrival in Florence through winter snow and it ends with his departure on a warm day in spring.

Prior to that point where the "irregular" border begins, a pattern of development is observable. The physical scene, the people, and the sounds of modern Florence are given the reader. These, in turn, contrast to a following brief summary of the Florentine past. General conclusions are drawn about the meaning of that history before the reader once again is brought to the present.

Having sketched a general background of past and present, Howells next considers individual characters and episodes in history which give rise to some realization or embody some truth about human nature. A house, a cathedral, a church, or a street commonly serves as a point from which an imaginative journey into the past may be taken. Once in the past, the narrator reenacts the drama of history, with the help of the reader if necessary. The mental adventurers then return to the anticlimax of the present. If they have visited a church famous for Savonarola's eloquent sermons, they hear, upon returning to the present, an Anglican preaching about "Agnosticism and the limitations of merely scientific wisdom" (p. 63). The balance of past and present, it might be noted, is only one aspect of the order evident in the essay. Howells also opposes such character types as Savonarola and Lorenzo and alternates between dramatic or narrative and expository modes.

When considering the nature of present Florentine society, Howells dispenses with obvious arrangement, as he promised he would. He does, however, touch upon several of the subjects he explored at greater length in *Venetian Life* and *Italian Journeys*. Briefly looking at such diverse but constant facts of existence as baptism, marriage, the theater, popular amusements, education, and civil authority, through his "scraps and shreds" he renders the character and variety of present Florence.

Evidently Howells liked the idea of using a metaphor to suggest his structure, for he utilized another in the second essay, "Panforte di Siene." He asserts that his haphazard structure can not hope to compete in quality with so excellent a confection as the famous Sienese panforte. This pastry, lavishly decorated with "a frosting of sugar, adorned broideries, with laces, with flowers, with leaves, with elegant figures in lively colors, and with artistic designs" (p. 136), attracts him because of its "chance and random associations of material" (p. 136).

In the briefer essays which conclude *Tuscan Cities*, Howells abandons any attempt to use a metaphor to suggest structure. He personifies Pisa, terms Lucca industrious, and merely names Pistoia, Prato, and Fiesole. When, on the final page, he steps aside to allow the reader a view of Florence (p. 251), a reader who, a few pages before, was not allowed to be a partner on the drive to Fiesole (p. 247), one realizes that his tired guide has been more than eager to close this account of Italian civilization.

The final essays on minor Tuscan cities suggest nothing so much as loose fragments and labored efforts. Since Howells depends on vivid figures to create interest, his account of these minor cities, deficient in notables as they are, can hardly escape being ineffectual. In them we find more surface detail with less perceivable relevance. The brevity of treatment may have been dictated, in part, by Howells anxiety about finishing *A Woman's Reason* (1883);[28] however, it also seems attributable to a dissatisfaction with his subject and methods. Perhaps his dissatisfaction also comes from an increasing awareness that his proper sphere of activity is not so much the past and its figures, but the "grotesque and burlesquing shadows we all cast while in the flesh" (p. 18).

At any rate, though one may feel, after reading the final essays, that the wonder of them is greater than the pleasure, he may have found adequate compensation in considering the possible implications arising from Howells' use of patterning metaphors. These metaphors, though static rather than organic in character, show Howells to be cautiously experimental. They also suggest a concern for possible relationships between art forms. The critic can hardly insist on the seriousness and functional adequacy of the metaphors, since his author does not. But he can not ignore them either.

Howells' admittedly light-hearted concern for two such minor art forms suggests that a rather more serious question may be in order: what modifications have occurred in his critical attitudes about more serious art? Even limited investigation shows that some changes have taken place. Clara Kirk rightly suggests that Howells, though still a professed amateur about matters of art, possessed a lively interest and a heightened sensitivity by the time of *Tuscan Cities*. Kirk further asserts that some of his descriptions seem "curiously suggestive of the French Impressionists then coming into vogue."[29] Though Howells does speak of impressionism, it is difficult to demonstrate a direct influence.

In *Tuscan Cities* he uses "impression" in a general rather than a technical sense. For example, he states that he attempts to create for the reader a "true impression of the sweet confusion of travel in those old lands" (p. 204). At another time he speaks of the difficulty of escaping a "crazy impression of intention in the spectacular prospect of Italy" (p. 56). A more instructive approach to the issue of pictorial elements in Howells' writing is through contrast. Two descriptive passages, one by James and one by Howells, will serve to focus on the issue. In the first Howells describes the countryside near Pisa:

> It was a plain country, and at this point a line of aqueduct stretched across the smiling fields to the horizon. There was something richly simple in the elements of the picture, which was of as few tones as a landscape of Titian or Raphael, and as strictly subordinated in its natural features to the human interest, which we did our best to represent. I dare say our best was but poor. Every acre of that plain had been the theatre of a great tragedy; every rood of ground had borne its hero. Now, in the advancing spring, the grass and the wheat were long enough to flow in the wind, and they flowed like the ripples of a wide green sea to the feet of those purple hills, away from our feet where we stood beside our carriage on its hither shore. The warmth of the season had liberated a fine haze that danced above the summer fields, and this quivered before us like the confluent phantoms of multitudes, indistinguishably vast, who had fallen there in immemorial strife. Yet we could not stand musing long upon this fact; we had taken the carriage by the hour. (p. 203)

James describes a view of Florence. "The view from Fiesole seems vaster and richer with each visit. The hollow in which Florence lies, and which from below seems deep and contracted, opens out into an immense and generous valley and leads away the eye into a hundred gradations of distance. The place itself showed, amid its chequered fields and gardens, with as many towers and spires as a chess-board half cleared. The domes and towers were washed over with a faint blue mist. The scattered columns of smoke interfused with the sinking sunlight, hung over them like streamers and pennons of silver gauze; and the Arno, twisting and curling and glittering here and there, was a serpent cross-striped with silver."[30]

James' description differs from Howells' primarily in an absence of generalization and in a greater emphasis upon the multiple objects composing the scene. James inclines to see landscape in terms of clearly perceived images; Howells looks for the human elements in it. James delights in "a hundred gradations of distance"; Howells prefers "richly simple" elements in his landscapes, as he does in art and architecture. He may see "inexhaustibly beautiful and delightful detail" (p. 172), as he does in the cathedral at Siena, but he declines to describe it. James, on the other hand, finds pleasure in fine shading and nuances of meaning suggested by manifold detail. One senses in James, as he does not in Howells, that the landscape has composed itself for the convenience of the image-making faculty, and that it has somehow taken on the form and flavor of his mind.

For Howells, art, as landscape, accrues value as it reflects the conditions of humanity or as it adapts itself to human needs. His eye does not linger on the prospect, or the art, before him, for one of the demands of his nature is that he be actively engaged with rapidly changing conditions. He may enjoy a fine landscape, but he also knows that he has taken the carriage by the hour. Thus though he can experience joy when viewing some paintings (p. 241), he can never lose himself in art (p. 76). He has too strong a sense of social significance to yield for long to the pursuit of pleasure or to the contemplation of aesthetic objects.

He expresses serious reservations about art which, to him, seems remote from man. He finds, for example, the interior of the Duomo in Florence a place which dampens "the spirit, dead or alive, by the immense impression of stony bareness, of drab vacuity, which one receives from its interior, unless it is filled with people" (p. 52). Though he finds the famous Four Fabrics of Pisa impressive, he still terms them deficient on two counts: they exist in isolation and fail in having no apparent function. Structures which are adapted to the use of men comprise, for Howells, "the last and finest effect of architecture" (p. 211). James, by way of contrast, does not insist on functional value, and agrees with a "happy remark of tasteful, old-fashioned Forsyth . . . as to the fact that the four famous objects are 'fortunate alike in their society and their solitude.' "[31]

Howells occasionally moves beyond a desire for functional appropriateness in architecture and for fidelity to life in painting. If what he sees has sufficient moral significance, it wins his approval. He finds a public palace in Florence "sacred" because he can associate it with the struggle of the democratic impulse to realize itself (pp. 79-80). In painting the human interest must be paramount or a picture fails to create its finest effect; if it does succeed, it still can not hope to compete with life. Early in *Tuscan Cities* Howells states that he would have rather had "the perpetuity of the *cameriere's* smile when he came up with our coffee in the morning than Donatello's San Giorgio, if either were purchasable; and the face of the old chamber-maid, Maria, full of motherly affection, was better than the facade of Santa Maria Novella" (p. 11).

Such statements as these have undoubtedly contributed to the notion that Howells possesses marginal aesthetic sensitivity. However, if seen less as reflections of an aesthetic position and more as indications of his concern with humanity, they are less apt to generate misunderstanding. More than anything, Howells implies that one neglects the humanity of the present in granting undue attention to the art of the past.

Other reservations about art entertained by Howells are referable to his bias for the social and the functional. These reservations, I feel, reflect a pragmatic attitude more than an anti-intellectual one. He more often complains about the methodology of art criticism than about the art he sees. He objects because such criticism insists that knowledge of technique is imperative to proper understanding; such insistence has the effect of rendering the experience of the viewer unimportant by substituting authority for it. Equally presumptuous to him are the demands of art critics that the viewer be well grounded in art history and concerned with the artists' intentions.

In reply to those who maintain that the gazer must have a knowledge of technique, Howells asserts that many works may be enjoyed by a man, "simply upon condition of his being a tolerably genuine human creature" (p. 118). He refuses to be academic about pictures; he has discovered that about art "others have spoken more than enough" (p. 118). Moreover, he finds it "worse than useless to be specific about pictures" (p. 184).

In emphatically denying that a knowledge of art history insures appreciation for the viewer, Howells ruefully considers how, in the Italy of his youth, he was victimized by his dependence upon the critical estimates of others. Again seeing some frescos by Orgagna, he remarks: "I had seen those Orgagna frescos before, and I had said to myself twenty years ago in obedience to whatever art critic I had in my pocket, that here was the highest evidence of the perfect sincerity in which the early masters wrought" (p. 208). Twenty years have also taught him that the aesthetic pilgrimages expected of a man of culture can be exercises in futility. Such a feeling probably prompted him to speak irritably of the "dreary old farce of old-master doing" (p. 79).

It is well to keep in mind that Howells directs his criticism more at the rigors of viewing than at the paintings. Early in the volume, in "shyly" renewing his acquaintance with the Florentine masters, he acknowledges that he has been made glad by the experience (p. 13). The great quantity of available art, however, may become an impediment. Thus, one who has only a moderate knowledge of art history, often finds himself victimized, a "miserable slave of the guidebook asterisks marking this or that thing as worth seeing" (p. 79). If one pays a few works adequate attention, he may expect continuing revelation. In seeing more paintings, one sees less in them.

If Howells senses the imaginative "spirit" informing the work under consideration (p. 13), he asks little more. This spirit is generally observable, if the artist has managed to capture some truth about human nature on his canvas. Howells carefully distinguishes between the spirit of a work and the sincerity or intention of the artist; the first can be discovered, the second only guessed at. Thus, Howells praises Lassels for not concerning himself with "the motives, or meanings, or aspirations" (p. 212) of the artists. Howells implies that to judge an artist's sincerity is absurd, for it can seldom be adequately established. Typically, when in Pisa, he wonders if those artists, whose works may be seen at the Campo Santo, "might not have worked with almost as little faith and reverence as so many American humorists" (p. 209). The art, rather than the beliefs of the artist, must primarily concern the viewer.

Since Howells concerns himself with the simple and the human in art, it seems appropriate that the illustrations in *Tuscan Cities* show these concerns. In Pennell's sketches, the reader sees the modern citizens of Italy in their natural costumes and conditions. When Howells stated his intentions for the travel book in a letter to Osgood, he also voiced his desire to avoid illustrations based on the work of past masters; he wished, instead, some which would show " 'life and character, past and present.' "[32] Those illustrations dealing with present life predominate.

In light of his desire for such illustrations, Stiles' assertion that Pennell's illustrations "unquestionably influenced the type of material Howells chose"[33] is debatable. No more verifiable is a suggestion by Kirk—to the effect that Pennell taught Howells to look for pictorial elements.[34] Forty years after Pennell did his sketches for *Tuscan Cities,* he wrote of his experience in Italy. Unfortunately, he says almost nothing about the working relationship he had with Howells. He merely suggests that some of the etchings he did were quite "good" and that he did all of them "out of doors."[35] He also cryptically comments that he "went about with Howells" to Siena, Pisa, and Pistoia.[36] But even without help from Pennell, one recognizes some connection between the text and the illustrations. However, since Howells nowhere suggests that he has accommodated his prose to the illustrator's sketches, one can make no very definite statements about influences. Save for the emphasis on history, he writes of many of the same aspects of Italian life he had written of twenty years before. The pictorial quality of his writing can be ascribed as justifiably to the novelist's heightened sensitivity to the scenes of life as to the influence of an illustrator. Finally, one can say that Howells asks of art what he strives for in prose: clarity, naturalness, and expressiveness.

The weight of evidence in *Tuscan Cities* points to the accuracy of Kirk's estimate of Howells' receptivity to art: his profound conviction about the value of "civilization" is in some measure dependent on his awareness of the relationships between the arts and the part each performs in depicting the realities of life.[37] Though not a connoisseur of art, in the sense that James is, he still elicits respect by virtue of his belief that art can, if it will, express man's highest aspirations.

What Howells discovers or affirms about art in *Tuscan Cities,* prefigures, in several ways, his expectations for art and the artist in Altruria. In this utopia, where brotherhood and cooperation are realities, art has a civilizing and humanizing function. Mr. Homos, in *A Traveler from Altruria* (1894), seemingly speaks for Howells when he discusses the nature of the arts and the responsibilities of the artist in Altruria:

> "When the labor of the community was emancipated from the bondage of the false to the free service of the true, it was also, by an inevitable implication dedicated to beauty and rescued from the old slavery to the ugly, the stupid, and the trivial. The thing that was honest and useful became, by the operation of a natural law, a beautiful thing. Once we had not enough time to make things beautiful, we were so overworked in making false and hideous things to sell; but now we had all the time there was, and a glad emulation arose among the trades and occupations to the end that everything done should be done finely as well as done honestly. The artist, the man of genius, who worked from the love of his work became the normal man, and in the measure of his ability and his calling each wrought in the spirit of the artist."[38]

Mr. Homos' beliefs are in several ways similar to those voiced by Howells in *Tuscan Cities*. Both accept a necessary relationship between function and form, use and beauty; both consider the spirit in which the artist creates to be significant—and believe that art can be a part of every man's life.

Tuscan Cities certainly shows Howells to be more than a frivolous tourist. The problems with form and technique which mar the book can not be attributed so much to a decline in his ability as to what might be termed a predicament of maturity. As an established novelist, critic, and defender of realism, he can not so easily use the approaches of two decades ago. A desire for recognition and an attack on the conventions of sentiment do not furnish him with primary motives for creation, as they seem to have done in *Venetian Life* and *Italian Journeys*. No more can the figures appearing on his pages serve the necessities of the picturesque. Art can not be so quickly repudiated nor embraced, nor can it be judged so absolutely.

If the Old World, in past or present dress, sometimes appears ridiculous, the student of human nature can not forget that men have been, and are, more like than unlike. Such a recognition by Howells accounts in part for both his increased tolerance and his skepticism. No longer an innocent abroad, he now sees a world which has increased in complexity and which makes greater demands upon the artist. Thus he may no longer ridicule, dismiss, or even accept what he imperfectly understands. A second Italian journey has forced him to reappraise his methods and attitudes about the travel experience. At a deeper level it has also led him to ponder the evident (and potential) darkness and cruelty in man.

If men are indeed more like than unlike, then Howells, in discovering evidence of this in others, past and present, has discovered some truths about himself. And the reader, if he has survived the jolts of some uneven travel, has also come to recognize that one begins to discover humanity once he has discovered some truths about himself. If Howells has prompted a part of this realization, then he may justly be credited with showing at least a modest genius for humanity.

NOTES

1. The chronology and details of Howells' trip are fully considered in James Woodress' *Howells & Italy*.
2. *Ibid.*, p. 177.

3. Firkins, p. 51.

4. W. D. Howells, *A Little Swiss Sojourn* (New York, 1892), p. 31. Subsequent references will be to this edition.

5. Cady, *The Road to Realism*, p. 221.

6. Woodress, p. 176.

7. *Ibid.*, p. 173.

8. W. D. Howells, *Tuscan Cities* (Boston, 1886), pp. 17-18. Subsequent references will be to this edition.

9. Woodress, p. 181. Woodress also maintains that *Tuscan Cities*, because it skilfully combines history and reporting, stands as "an apotheosis of travel literature."

10. [Review of Henry James' *Transatlantic Sketches*], *Atlantic Monthly*, XXXVI (July 1875), 113. Albert Mordell attributes this review to Howells in *Discovery of a Genius: William Dean Howells and Henry James,* ed. Albert Mordell (Montpelier, Vermont, 1961), p. 71. However, William Gibson and George Arms do not list it in *A Bibliography of William Dean Howells* (New York, 1948), and possibly the attribution is doubtful.

11. W. D. Howells, *Indian Summer*, intro. William M. Gibson (New York, 1958). In *Indian Summer*, Howells has Mr. Waters voice a similar concern for the realizations of history when he speaks to Colville: " 'The past is humanity set free from circumstance, and history studied where it was once life is the past rehumanized' " (p. 180).

12. [William Dean Howells, "The New Historical Romances," *North American Review*, CLXXI (December 1900), 942-43.] Quoted by Carter, *Howells and The Age of Realism*, p. 61. By 1900 Howells was asking nature's cooperation, for he was working on *The Leatherwood God* (1916), a historical novel in which he successfully re-creates the past of the Ohio frontier.

13. Howells also suggests his ambivalence about the past in his review of James' *Transatlantic Sketches*. He finds James ably capturing the sense of "mingled pain and happiness" which is the visitor's lot in Europe. While the American can find pleasure in the Old World, he cannot consider it home: "we do not and cannot belong to it, nor it to us" (p. 113).

14. W. D. Howells, *Life in Letters of William Dean Howells*, ed. Mildred Howells, 2 vols. (Garden City, N.Y., 1928), I, 338.

15. Kirk, *Howells and Art*, p. 189. The essays which make up *Criticism and Fiction* appeared in *Harper's Monthly* between 1886-90.

16. W. D. Howells, "Editor's Study," *Harper's Monthly*, LXXV (September 1887), 639.

17. W. D. Howells, "A New Observer," *Atlantic Monthly*, XLV (June 1880), 849.

18. *Ibid.*, p. 848.

19. Mr. Waters, in *Indian Summer*, expresses a similar view when he con-

cludes: " 'There is something very mysterious in what we call evil. Apparently it has infinitely greater force and persistence than good. I don't know why it should be so. But so it appears' " (p. 182).

20. Howells, *Indian Summer*, p. 180.

21. Robert Penn Warren, "A Lesson Read in American Books," *The New York Times Book Review*, December 11, 1955, Sec. 7, p. 33.

22. Firkins, p. 45.

23. Stiles, p. 100.

24. Cooke, pp. 136-37.

25. Howells appears to be both attracted and repelled by the stories of the Florentine past. He says of them: "Terrible stories, which I must try to excuse myself for telling the thousandth time. At least I did not invent them" (*TC*, p. 86).

26. Howells' interest in skeptical thought is revealed in *A Little Swiss Sojourn* by the attention he devotes to St. Bonivard. This "cheerful sceptic" (p. 35) appeals to him because his skepticism was inspired by his "knowledge of the human heart" (p. 30).

27. W. D. Howells, "Editor's Study," *Harper's Monthly*, LXII (January 1886), 325.

28. Woodress, p. 176.

29. Kirk, *Howells and Art*, p. 86.

30. James, *Italian Hours*, pp. 282-83.

31. *Ibid.*, p. 311.

32. Kirk, *Howells and Art*, p. 82.

33. Stiles, p. 67.

34. Kirk, *Howells and Art*, pp. 83-84.

35. Joseph Pennell, "Adventures of an Illustrator: with Howells in Italy," *Century*, CIV (May 1922), 140.

36. *Ibid.*, p. 141.

37. Kirk, *Howells and Art*, p. 94.

38. W. D. Howells, *A Traveler from Altruria*, intro. Howard Mumford Jones (New York, 1957), p. 185.

4

OBLIGATIONS TO
CONSCIOUSNESS

When in London in 1904, Howells chanced to see John Dryden's house. Unexpected tears came to his eyes. He had no particular affection for Dryden as a poet, yet he recognized an instant claim on his attention, merely because the writer was English. The experience led him to conclude: "It is but one of a thousand names, great in some sort or other, which make sojourn in London impossible, if one takes them to heart as an obligation to consciousness of her constant and instant charm."[1] He might have said the same for the whole of England. *London Films* (1906), *Certain Delightful English Towns* (1906), and *Seven English Cities* (1909) reflect the particular obligations to consciousness felt by the travel writer in England.

These obligations arise primarily from Howells' awareness of the inexhaustible richness of English life and history; but they also stem from his knowledge of prior treatment of "our old home" by such American writers as Emerson, Hawthorne, and James. Contrast, Howells maintains, serves as the "only basis for inference" (*LF*, p. 10). Thus in London he carries about a "pocket vision" of New York. Similarly, I will draw inferences about Howells by contrasting present techniques to the techniques found in his earlier travel accounts

and by contrasting his account of English life to those by James, Hawthorne, and Emerson.

The problems of technique Howells encountered (and created) in
Tuscan Cities arose primarily from his desire to come to terms with
the past and at the same time to express his altruistic impulses. He
appears to have solved these problems in his three books on England.
Though he treats dramatic incidents as frequently as before, they are
less marked by strenuous activity: realization of the past by imaginative participation has been discarded as a device. Though past and
present jostle each other constantly in England, the tension between
them has lessened. He does not treat the past as frequently, and when
he does, he often looks at it humorously or treats it with a fancy that
does not strain for effects. Instead of drawing moral lessons from the
actions of figures in the past, he now displays an interest in historical
continuity and in the institutions and objects emblematic of this continuity.

Unevenness in point of view, which plagued him earlier, no longer
does so. He assigns appropriate voices to both the narrator and the
omniscient author. He still employs the familiar address, but inclines
to be kinder to his audience than he was in *Tuscan Cities*.

He shows greater facility in handling images than in his earlier
books. He uses more of them, quite unobtrusively, and in some in-
stances he sustains them remarkably well. Images which were static
in *Tuscan Cities* function more as covert symbols in the English
books.[2] In their rich suggestiveness and complex interaction, they
skilfully underscore the dense texture of English life—a primary
theme in each of the volumes. Howells' use of images, as a means of
indirectly making a thematic statement, marks a significant advance
in his ability as a travel writer.

Characteristically, Howells is modest about his abilities, and he
anticipates possible questions about the comparative value of his
volumes and Emerson's *English Traits*. Emerson's study of English
character, he concludes, "makes all other comment seem idle and
superfluous palaver."[3] Daniel apparently accepts Howells' estimate.
Though she finds Emerson and Howells in agreement "on many

points relative to the English character and variety,"[4] she concludes that Howells' observations are "not of deep significance."[5] Cady suggests something of the same sort. He quite accurately finds Howells to be at the peak of his travel writing career: Howells has, "in *London Films* and *Certain Delightful English Towns*, 1906, his own interpretations of Britain to set beside Emerson's *English Traits*."[6] But Cady also finds Howells writing for the market[7] and tending toward "a suave but tired impressionism."[8] In spite of Howells' modest disclaimer and his critics' reservations, I feel his books can be placed beside Emerson's without undue embarrassment. Though he has not attempted so much as Emerson, he has not been so often victimized by a theory.

If slight attention has been paid to possible connections between Emerson and Howells, less has been said of Hawthorne's influence.[9] Such neglect is ironic, particularly since *Our Old Home* appears to influence Howells more than *English Traits*. Howells' consistent interest in taking mental possession of various English homes hints humorously at his indebtedness. Most especially, Hawthorne's volume appears to have suggested to Howells some useful metaphors; through these he evokes his central thematic concerns. He has none of Hawthorne's relish for mouldering graveyards, little of his inclination for speculative psychology or morality, and only a slight tendency toward the allegorical method. However, they share a skeptical habit of mind and a healthy interest in social and economic conditions. On occasion Howells' ideas and approaches appear to be directly influenced by *Our Old Home*.

The extent of James' influence on Howells is more difficult to assess. As an admirer of James, Howells must certainly have been aware of the appearance of his friend's travel essays about England in the 1870's and 80's. Yet he nowhere alludes to these essays, which when gathered made up *English Hours* (1905), and beyond the fact that both writers use a method which can be termed "impressionistic," few similarities can be insisted upon. Still, to have a method in common is to have very much in common. George Arms, in his treatment of technique in Howells' English books, suggests that a primary concern of Howells is "to convey" the impressions he has fought for. He also suggests Howells' probable indebtedness to James for the conception of the impression as a means of verifying reality.[10] A comparative study of impressionistic technique yields worthwhile conclusions about the affinities between realism and impressionism. It also suggests much about the "impressionism" that each uses to convey his sense of reality.

Early in *London Films* Howells suggests the extent of his involvement with England; he casually mentions that he has just asked himself "what he honestly thought and felt about this England which he had always been more or less bothering about" (p. 78). The "newest Americans" see England as they never can in later years. As Howells notes, "they are apt to see it in the measure of that simplicity for which sincerity is by no means a satisfactory substitute."[11] Unlike the "newest Americans," who unconsciously see much of England and little of themselves, Howells knows more of himself and Americans and readily acknowledges that he knows less of England. Hawthorne, in *Our Old Home*, had earlier confessed that he too learned much of American character after he became American Consul in Liverpool.[12] He further acknowledged that the new American is capable of seeing England with a freshness not possible to the island's natives.[13]

Greater familiarity with a foreign country evidently has the effect of increasing one's awareness of the difficulties inherent in understanding it. Thus when Howells notes that the English often sequester themselves behind formidable hedges, he also states: "Americans are very penetrating, and I would not be sure that the thickest and highest hedge was invulnerable to them" (*SEC*, p. 9). Howells' statement echoes Hawthorne, who found the English hedge and fence accurate emblems of "the careful exclusiveness of the English character."[14] Howells, however, goes beyond Hawthorne in implying the difficulties of estimating that character.

The traveler, who touches upon the "surfaces and edges of life" (*CDET*, p. 190) can not be expected to penetrate very deeply. Yet he can not wholly evade the necessity of judging. In the books of English travels Howells is cautious and more judicious than he was in his earlier works. The emphatic moral tone of *Venetian Life* and

Italian Journeys has vanished, and the explicit altruism of *Tuscan Cities* has diminished. Howells has resolved "to practice that slowness in sentencing and executing offenders against one's native ideals which has always been the conspicuous ornament of English travelers among ourselves" (*CDET*, p. 91).

His "slowness in sentencing" might have struck Emerson as evasive. The transcendentalist condemns the English because they "shrink from a generalization."[15] Certainly Emerson rarely shrinks from one. A brief look at some features of Emerson's generalizations will serve to show how different they are from Howells'. While Emerson does admit to "difficulty in making a social or moral estimate of England,"[16] he still "estimates" with a degree of assurance not common in Howells' books. If England, as he asserts, "subsists by antagonisms and contradictions,"[17] then opposing generalizations are legitimate, even expected. He presents these generalizations convincingly. They are made convincing, in part, by being often yoked to a simple, concrete fact, or by being conveyed by vigorous verbs and sharp metaphors. Emerson concludes, for example, that "Steam is almost an Englishman."[18] Or he observes that the English "kiss the dust before a fact."[19]

Emerson's generalizations usually keep their feet on the ground, and irony and humor often provide a necessary ballast. After remarking that the English have an oppressive bias toward the utilitarian, he predicts that they possibly "will teach spiders to weave silk stockings."[20] At another point he concludes: "The religion of England is part of good breeding."[21] However, irony, humor, concreteness, and direct vigor do not necessarily insure reliability. His conclusions, though often acute (as Howells observes), are occasionally questionable because they are excessively influenced by a theory. His inclination to find contraries is symptomatic of this kind of influence, as is his theoretical interest in what might be termed "cultural anthropology." He criticizes Robert Knox because he "did not found his assumed races on any necessary law, disclosing their ideal or metaphysical necessity."[22] Emerson demonstrates throughout *English Traits* that his generalizations serve this "metaphysical necessity."

When Howells generalizes about England he is nearer James than

Emerson. James finds London proving false "any generalization you may have been so simple as to make about it."[23] Howells, in similar fashion, terms it "an irresolvable and immense question" (LF, p. 44). Howells often expresses his unwillingness to hazard questionable generalizations. He explicitly voices reservations about the accuracy of his judgments, as he does when he contrasts American and English social attitudes: "The sensibilities are more spared in the one [England] and the self-respect in the other [America], though this is saying it too loosely, and may not be saying it truly" (LF, p. 25). At other times, as Arms observes, he may project "his generalizations as those of a narrator rather than of omniscient author."[24] Such generalizations do not so much assert as they suggest the possibilities for more exhaustive exploration.

The generalizations to which Howells hesitates to give full authority suggest the importance of indirection and implication in his method. He hints at his preference for such a method in *Certain Delightful English Towns;* he announces in somewhat humorous terms that he wishes "to be at ease in the large freedom of the truth rather than bound in a slavish fidelity to the fact" (pp. 66-67). Facts, he observes, may hinder the "enjoyment of the moment's chances" (LF, p. 142). Truth's freedom, it appears, rests in neither fact nor generalization. Howells shares Emerson's distaste for great quantities of facts. He complains of "suffocating" London facts (LF, p. 193) for example,[25] while Emerson criticizes the English for piling up "heaps of facts"[26] —a practice wholly negative and uncongenial to the poetic faculty. Yet for Emerson a fact can be "an Epiphany of God,"[27] and he shows a healthy interest in facts. The ship on which Emerson sailed to England, the reader discovers, "was registered 750 tons, and weighed perhaps, with all her freight, 1500 tons. The mainmast, from the deck to the top-button, measured 115 feet; the length of the deck, from stem to stern, 155."[28]

Howells can not acknowledge a necessary connection between fact and spiritual truth. Early in *London Films* he observes that there is probably "relative fact" rather than "positive fact" (p. 10). He may use facts to keep his feet on the ground, as he does when he is in danger of ecstasy at the Henley races (*LF*, p. 172), but he will not insist upon the sociological or scientific accuracy of his observed facts (*LF*, p. 3). He may even suggest that a "want of definition in the fact" may increase its value (*LF*, p. 25).

Howells' inclination to see relative fact and to use tentative generalization could suggest a deficiency in perception. The inclination can be more profitably understood, however, as symptomatic of the complexity of his perspectives. His attitudes incline to be plural and his method pragmatic. He can consider the "question" of England without the necessity of solving it, for such a solution would be presumptuous. A frank admission of ambivalence has the merit of freeing him from the bondage of final statement. He suggests that he was never an enemy of the "confusion of the old and the new" in Europe (*CDET*, p. 35). He frequently questions the reality of what he has seen, and even concludes, for example, that about York he "need not be so very definite" in what he knows (*SEC*, p. 51).

Though Howells denies himself the luxury of definitive statement, he also recognizes the limitations of wholly personal or primarily subjective observation. To impart weight to his observations, he often presents them as characteristic—those of a typical traveler.[29] (In like manner Hawthorne feels obligated to try to find "some characteristic feature" which will convey his sense of English antiquity.[30]) The generalizations advanced by a typical traveler may have in them a kind of truth that arises from common experience. On the other hand, Howells admits that travel may lead one astray insofar as it encourages seeking the typical and thereby neglecting "immediate examples" (*CDET*, p. 20). Balance between the typical and the immediate is necessary.

More than in his earlier travel accounts Howells concerns himself with the processes and consequences of method; however, the subject matter he treats remains essentially unchanged. As in past volumes, he declines to describe architecture or to criticize art. And again he refuses to be "sordidly and rapaciously concerned with objects of interest" (*SEC*, p. 16). People of interest are another thing altogether.

Though he terms his perspectives "polite" (*LF*, p. 42), they are not wholly so. More often than not they serve the purpose of contrast. He views the despair of "low" life (*LF*, pp. 112-13) and the "antic aspects" (*LF*, p. 196) as often as he touches upon the manners of polite society. In *London Films* he abruptly ends his discussion of "society" because he can not continue to celebrate the London season—"that great moment in the social life of a vast empire" (p. 54)—without charging himself with hypocrisy.

A "lover of dramatic incident" (*CDET*, p. 66), he most often records the small dramatic happenings of common people, as Arms notes.[31] Because he makes free only with "simple life" (*SEC*, p. 76) and deals with "plebians" like himself, he suspects that he will be labeled a "bigoted realist" (*LF*, p. 93). A "student of human nature" and a "lover of mild adventure" (*LF*, p. 77), he does not pretend that his studies or adventures lead him to an overwhelming Prufrockian question. Yet to a surprising degree, his supposedly limited investigations do lead him toward valuable conclusions about such things as the uses of tradition and the causes and effects of social injustices.

In *London Films* Howells expresses his concern for the poor in a chapter entitled "Glimpses of the Lowly and the Lowlier," with a probable allusion to a chapter in *Our Old Home* called "Outside Glimpses of English Poverty." He squarely considers drunkenness, misery, and poverty. He also wryly notes that in London he has seen less of the "misery that indecently obtrudes itself upon prosperity" than he has in New York (p. 111). When he can not bring himself to condemn women drinkers who may be "merely relieving in that moment of liquored leisure the long weariness of the week's work" (p. 109), he again appears to echo Hawthorne. Hawthorne suspected the "sad revellers" he saw to be in need of a fiery stimulant "to lift them a little way out of the smothering squalor of both their outward and interior life."[32]

A memorable instance of Howells' ability to dramatize both his guilt and his concern for the poverty-stricken occurs in *London Films*. He offers a shilling to a man "down on his luck." In concluding about the affair he states: "If his need had apparently been less dire I might have made it a sovereign; but one must not fly in the face of Providence, which is probably not ill-advised in choosing certain of us to be reduced to absolute destitution. The man smiled a sick, thin-lipped smile which showed his teeth in a sort of pinched way, but did not speak more; his wife, gloomily unmoved, passed me without a look, and I rather slunk back to my seat, feeling that I had represented, if I had not embodied, society to her" (p. 113). Howells avoids overt moralism by presenting the scene through the eyes of a narrator, yet in suggesting that he represents an unjust social system, he attaches a general significance to the experience.

Though Howells has his eye most often on the human elements of England, he does not neglect other material. He delights in the beauty of the English landscapes; birds, trees, flowers, hedges, gardens—all evoke fresh responses from an aging traveler. The objects of the natural world often become emblematic of English life. Perhaps Howells had at the back of his mind Emerson's suggestion that "the views of nature held by any people determine all their institutions."[33] If Howells looks more often at nature in his English books than he did in the Italian ones, he less frequently deals with the facts of history. To domestic affairs, accommodations, and lodgings he devotes more attention than would be warranted, were it not that his investigations of railway hotels, thatched huts, country houses, cottages, and town houses provide clues about the character and dimensions of the larger ancestral home he seeks.

"The merit of England," Emerson concludes, is that it is "well packed and well saved."[34] Howells, however, sees less positive merit in such packing and saving, for the abundant material available to the traveler frequently proves a hindrance to his perceptions and his emotions. As a consequence, Howells' primary obligations are to the passing effects of a fluid world rather than to the solid but insoluble facts of English civilization. The inconclusive and the transient often distract him from such facts. In London, typically enough, he announces that he must defer an inquiry into "English civilizations" because of a passing effect which has caught his eye (LF, p. 78). He roughly records these effects "in behalf of a futile philosopher who ought to have studied them in their inexhaustible detail" (*LF*, p. 78). This futile philosopher, of course, is Howells, who knows quite as well as his reader that he has seldom concerned himself with inexhaustible detail. He admits that he could have been "very graphic" about Marston Moor—if he had somehow managed to find it (*SEC*, p. 71).

Passing effects can be seen with less difficulty than Marston Moor, and to convey his sense of these Howells employs the impression. As early as *Venetian Life* and *Italian Journeys* he had used the device; however, it did not appear a dominant feature of his method. Now it does. He alludes to it so often that his reader can not fail to grasp its import. The device of impression served Henry James equally well for recording the elusive nature of reality in England, as one familiar with his *English Hours* (1905) can attest.

The methods of the two impressionists are quite different, as even the most casual glance at the two following passages reveals. James describes the "truths" of his beloved London, a "murky, modern Babylon":

They colour the thick, dim distances which in my opinion are the most romantic town-vistas in the world; they mingle with the troubled light to which the straight ungarnished aperture in one's dull, undistinctive housefront affords a passage and which makes an interior of friendly corners, mysterious tones and unbetrayed ingenuities, as well as with the low, magnificent medium of the sky, where the smoke and fog and the weather in general, the strangely undefined hour of the day and season of the year, the emanations of industries and the reflection of furnaces, the red gleams and blurs that may or may not be of sunset . . . all hang together in a confusion, a complication, a shifting but irremovable canopy. They form the undertone of the deep perpetual voice of the place.[35]

Howells attempts to suggest some "qualities" of London:

There are certain characteristics, qualities, of London which I am aware of not calling aright, but which I will call *sentiments* for want of some better word. One of them was the feel of the night air, especially late in the season, when there was a waste and weariness in it as if the vast human endeavor for pleasure and success had exhaled its despair upon it. Whatever there was of disappointment in one's past, of apprehension in one's future, came to the surface of the spirit, and asserted its unity with the collective melancholy. . . . Through the senses it related itself to the noises of the quiescing city, to the smell of its tormented dust, to the whiff of a casual cigar, or the odor of the herbage and foliage in the park or square that one was passing, [sic] one may not be more definite about what was perhaps nothing at all. (LF, p. 229)

Both passages are effective, though for very different reasons. James emphasizes the visual experience; nothing precise is seen, however, for he wishes to impart a sense of the confusion of the atmosphere rather than to delineate precisely the objects he sees. Such phrases as "troubled light," "magnificent medium," "gleams and blurs," and "emanations" are purposely abstract and even vague. With the word "canopy" James finally closes the scene on a more concrete note. The mingling, confusion, and complication which constitute the visual experience are subtly reinforced by the complex, somewhat loose sentence pattern he employs.

Howells creates his effect by skilfully contrasting general, abstract diction to the sharper, more concrete language seen in the last few lines. Howells uses no visual images. His form does not reflect the content as James' does. The vague personification of "endeavor" and the suggestion of representative experience ("collective melancholy") are neatly balanced by the more concrete, if yet elusive, character of casual cigar smoke and tormented dust. By using sensory experience to reflect emotional and mental experience, Howells deftly creates a sense of something which was "perhaps nothing at all."

On occasion Howells fails to convey adequately his impressions. Generalizations overshadow visual or imaginative elements, and observation gives way to speculation. At such times he often brings a fact or characteristic to a character rather than observing it in him, as we see in the following passage: "The very handsomest man I saw, with the most perfectly patrician profile (if we imagine something delicately aquiline to be patrician), was a groom who sat his horse beside Rotten Row, waiting till his master should come to command the services of both. He too had the look of long descent, but if it could not be said that he had cost the nation too much time and money, it might still be conjectured that he had cost some one too much of something better" (*LF*, p. 45). Such words and phrases as "imagine," "a look of," and "might still be conjectured" indicate Howells' willingness to go beyond available information. Perhaps Howells hints at illicit love and the illegitimacy of the groom, but the hint is a slight one.

On the whole, however, Howells' impressions succeed by virtue of their evident imagination and freshness. They seem finely unpremeditated. Manifestations of conscious mental process are not obvious in his prose, though, more than ever, Howells associates the impression with conscious perceptual activity. He still delights in incidental or chance impressions, but he more actively searches for other impressions. In *London Films*, for example, he speaks of deliberately and hopefully setting out with his "sensitized surfaces" (mental films) to capture an impression of a "certain historic spectacle" (p. 27). In *Seven English Cities* he humorously speaks of the disappointment of an "aesthetic visitor" who is denied his impression because a Manchester mill can not be started up for his sole pleasure (p. 22).

The impressions Howells records are not so elaborately sustained or lovingly relished as those James pursues. When speaking of Liverpool, James admits his delight in having "an exclusive property in the impression. I prolonged it, I sacrificed to it, and it is perfectly recoverable now. . . . "[36] While perhaps the intensity and duration of an impression may account for its "recoverability," James implies, through his method, the necessity for amplifying and arranging it to achieve its finest effect. His reader can not escape the realization that James has carefully composed the scene, exquisitely shaped the material.

Though James observes, when discussing the countryside around Chester, that "English landscape is always a 'landscape with figures,' "[37] his impressions less often involve individual figures than do Howells'. Howells, to cite a typical example, observes "three tall young Hindoos, in native dress, and white-turbaned to their swarthy foreheads, who suddenly file out of the crowd, looking more mystery from their liquid eyes than they could well have corroborated in word or thought, and bring to the metropolis of the West the gorgeous and foolish magnificence of the sensuous East" (*LF*, p. 45). This impression, as Howells soon after concludes, "was of far greater duration than that of most individual impressions of the London crowd" (p. 47). Such a conclusion is symptomatic of his preference for impressions which emphasize figures more than landscape, a specific incident rather than a sense of general activity. James more often presents a large view, as we see in the following description of crowds in a London railway station: "The exhibition of variety of type is in general one of the bribes by which London induces you to condone her abominations, and the railway platform is a kind of compendium of that variety. I think that nowhere so much as in London do people wear—to the eye of observation—definite signs of the sort of people they may be. If you like above all things to know the sort, you hail this fact with joy; you recognize that if the English are immensely distinct from other people they are also socially—and that brings with it, in England, a train of moral and intellectual consequences—extremely distinct from each other."[38]

This distinctiveness of character finds a limited place in his own accounts. London, on the other hand, is personified. A mystery and a monster, the city is even more a "she." James anticipates his portrait of Aunt Maud in *The Wings of the Dove* when he describes London in 1888: "Excess is her highest reproach, and it is her incurable misfortune that there is really too much of her. She overwhelms you by quantity and number—she ends by making human life, by making civilisation, appear cheap to you."[39] She overwhelms Howells also, but human life never appears cheap to him. So small a thing as the kindness an older child shows a younger catches the eye of the mild adventurer, and he concludes: "nothing, no spotting or thick plastering of filth, can obscure their inborn sweetness" (*LF*, p. 94).

Not only must Howells contend with the "quantity and number" of English things standing between him and his impression but he must also deal with past impressions. He remarks that "first images of places always remain, however blurred and broken, and the Temple gardens were a dim and fractured memory in the retrospect as I next saw them" (*LF*, p. 96). Only rarely does an advantage accrue to the traveler, whose repeated perspectives thicken rather than clear the air about an object. One of the few advantages is "that all experiences become more or less contemporaneous, and that at certain moments you can not be distinctly aware just when and where you are" (*LF*, p. 205). The humor implicit in the admission suggests that he finds the advantage a small one.

Frequently Howells complains of his inability to treat adequately the fragile, fleeting, and evanescent aspects of experience. When discussing his journey to Oxford, he concludes that the will can not impart the "finer impressions of such a place" (*CDET*, p. 217). At another time he regrets that such fleeting glimpses as he sees "leave only a blurred record upon the most receptive mind" (*LF*, p. 47).

The "blurred record" and coarse impressions which Howells seems fated to record, however, suggest much more than merely the difficulty of an observer. They suggest that for him sensory and subjective experience has increased in complexity and value; he values his impressions enough to fight for them (*CDET*, p. 173). In his commitment to them he resembles James, who in his "Preface" to *The American Scene* passionately concludes: "I would take my stand upon my gathered impressions, since it was all for them, for them only, that I returned; I would in fact go to the stake for them—which is a sign of the value that I both in particular and in general attach to them and that I have endeavoured to preserve for them in this transcription."[40] Leon Edel suggests that James speaks from deep feeling, and "we do well to listen."[41] We do well to listen to Howells also.

Howells' distrust of the utility and value of facts has apparently increased over the years. Consequently, he accords the impression, though fragile, a larger role. It can rescue him from the heavy obligations of fact and at the same time suggest something of the totality of experience. When, in *Seven English Cities*, Howells sees a fox hunt, he humorously suggests that he now has a complete "impression of English society" (p. 90). The comment illustrates his use of a technique which can most readily and practically treat the irreducible complexities of English life. It also shows him having a little fun at the expense of the aristocratic and romantic novel.

As earlier suggested, Howells uses images more effectively than he did in his Italian books. Often his images and his impressions are closely related. He most explicitly suggests their interrelatedness during a visit to Oxford. Faced with an inexhaustible wealth of impressions, Howells admits that he must be content to reveal "mere fragmentary glimpses of the fact, broken lines, shattered images, blurred colors" (CDET, p. 197). He appears to value some impressions and images above others. He prizes first images or impressions because of their intensity. Others which appear with enough frequency to acquire symbolic value afford him the means for a strategy of indirection.

A primary image in *London Films* is the "flood of life." The figure is not particularly original, for James had used it in his 1888 essay on London. Hyde Park corner, James asserts, shows a great "flood of life." He extends the figure by speaking of the rhythm of "waves of traffic," and of a slackening current.[42] Howells uses the figure to impart his sense of the great rush of London traffic, but also to suggest the immense vitality and productivity of London. After discussing the transiency of any individual impression of London street life, Howells likens the impression to a "shimmering facet of a specific wavelet" which in such a flood seems an insignificant "ripple in a river" (p. 47).

Other important images are also closely associated with multiple impressions. London smoke, for example, forms "a solution in which all associations were held, and from which they were, from time to time, precipitated in specific memories" (p. 122). Perhaps there is, in this figure, an oblique reference to the process of film development; at any rate it points to Howells' concern for extractive process. Specific impressions are often precipitated from a solution of experience. Fog and mist, as well as smoke, serve Howells as metaphors of experience which continually shift and change.

Image and impression appear to interact complexly: "The impressions were all, if I may so try to characterize them, transitory; they were effects of adventitious circumstances; they were not structural in their origin. The most memorable aspect of The Strand or Fleet Street would not be its moments of stately architecture, but its moments of fog or mist, when its meanest architecture would show stately. The city won its moving grandeur from the throng of people astir on its pavements, or the streams of vehicles solidifying and liquefying in its streets" (*LF*, p. 133). The passage illustrates his interest in the unstructured nature of experience—its fluidity, and its momentary character. It also implies his interest in giving his reader a sense of active experience.

Just as complex relationships exist between image and impression, so do they between image clusters. The cumulative effect of the images Howells uses depends in large measure on the memories they recall for the reader, the reverberations they set up, and the echoes they sound. Because his images are finely suggestive, they seem particularly appropriate to impart a sense of the dense texture of English civilization.

Of the images Howells uses, those of texture and growth—water, smoke, haze, fog, mist, foliage, flowers, and trees—are primary. Others of importance are images of movement, stability, and continuity. He draws most of his images from the natural world. When he uses others, they are often associated with nature. Because of their abundance, one can do no more than point to a few of the reciprocities existing between them.

Early in *London Films* Howells voices his appreciation of the natural world (p. 8). He playfully attributes to London certain features of nature: "London is like nature in its vastness, simplicity, and deliberation, and if it hurried or worried, it would be like the precession of the equinoxes getting a move on, and would shake the earth" (pp. 102-03). He not only finds London like nature; he also finds many manifestations of the natural world in it, as he does throughout England. Birds, for example, are a constant feature of English life whose presence and song he gratefully acknowledges (*LF*, p. 125). He frequently hears them singing in the mist (*LF*, p. 84)—a mist which appears of much the same density as the trees. At one point he expresses a symbolic intent. He discovers that English birds perform more authoritatively than their American cousins "and find an echo in the mysterious depths of our ancestral past where they and we are compatriots" (*CDET*, p. 11). Generally, however, Howells does not so directly suggest a specific meaning for either the birds or their song. The "meaning" grows gradually from the frequent references to the birds throughout the pages. Rooks in particular catch his attention, and on several occasions are associated with harvest and growth.

In *English Traits* Emerson early concludes that "England is a garden."[43] He later modifies his statement, and suggests that it is an "over-cultivated garden" from which the "great-mother" has been driven.[44] Hawthorne and Howells find much the same condition, though both go beyond Emerson's terse judgments. Hawthorne, for example, does not find the absence of the mother particularly annoying. He finds the charm of the English countryside residing in the "rich verdure of the fields, in the stately wayside trees and carefully kept plantations of wood, and in the old and high cultivation that has humanized the very sods by mingling so much of man's toil and care among them. To an American there is a kind of sanctity even in an English turnip field. . . ."[45] He does, however, recognize the great disparity between luxuriant English nature and the "rude, shaggy, barbarous nature" of America.[46]

Though Howells is as much concerned about the cultivation of the soil and the humanization of the natural world as Hawthorne, he treats the idea of England as a garden more indirectly. He finds it convenient, for example, to discuss persons of fashion as "flowers" (*LF*, p. 44) or as "bright birds" (*LF*, p. 179). The apparent confusion of the artificial and the natural is the point. What could be less natural to a democratic American than persons of fashion? Yet what could be more natural to England? The difficulty the American has in distinguishing the natural from the artificial is a primary symptom of the larger confusion which it is his peculiar fate to enjoy when in England. Howells insists upon this confusion more in *Seven English*

Cities than in the other two volumes; he easily mistakes sun and mist (p. 89), and the seasons strike him as confused beyond understanding. In all three volumes, however, he distinguishes between past and present, dream and actuality, with difficulty. So great is the danger that at one point he momentarily mistakes a statue of George III for George Washington (*LF*, p. 136). It hardly seems surprising then that the images of the natural world partake of this larger confusion. However, they also suggest it as a main thematic thread.

Images of growth appear, as one would expect, in Howells' descriptions of the countryside, parks, and gardens, but they also are associated with such man-made structures as churches, cathedrals, and towers. He finds a Gothic church in Bath "in a gracious sort of harmony with itself through its lovely proportions; and from the stems of its clustered columns the tracery of their fans spreads and delicately feels its way over the vaulted roof as if it were a living growth of something rooted in the earth beneath" (*CDET*, p. 52). Hawthorne advances a similar conception of harmony. When describing the cathedral at Lichfield, he terms the Gothic the "most wonderful work of man." He further finds its intricacy and profound simplicity "so consonant" that "it ultimately draws the beholder and his universe into its harmony."[47] Hawthorne finds this simplicity and universality a product of "those simple ages when men 'builded better than they knew.' "[48] If Howells can not find a beholder's universe in a cathedral, he finds that the principle dictating its structure and significance comes from nature. The Gothic, in a sense, is nature given permanent form; its harmony is a natural expression—an expression from the soil. Howells' love of the Gothic is hardly new, nor is his inclination to describe it in terms of images drawn from nature. Nevertheless, his attitudes appear to be more complex than in the past, and they point more insistently toward an interest in organic form.

A few examples will further serve to illustrate his concern for relationships between growth and structures or institutions. He terms the Canterbury Cathedral, which he sees surrounded by blossoms, "a vast efflorescence of the age of faith, mystically beautiful in form, and gray as some pale exhalation from the mould of the ever cloistered, the deeply reforested past" (*CDET*, p. 177). The towers of Oxford he sees as a "petrified efflorescence of the past, lovelier than any new May-wrought miracle of leaf and flowers" (*CDET*, p. 193).

Typically, however, he refuses to take with complete seriousness the connections he establishes. When at Oxford he interrogates a certain shrub and discovers that it does not exist "specifically"; it exists as an "herbacious expression of the University" (*CDET*, p. 214). In *London Films*, he gently ridicules his tendency to use so often the idea of growth. Some English giants, he concludes, "were doubtless the result of a natural selection to which money for buying perfect conditions had contributed as much as the time necessary for growing a type" (p. 43). On the whole, however, he is more serious. The tone of his description of the cathedral at Exeter is more representative. The cathedral strikes him as an example of something which has "continued to grow, like living things, from the hearts rather than the hands of strongly believing men" (*CDET*, p. 22).

Howells treats growth more frequently in *Certain Delightful English Towns* than in the other English books; his interest in the subject, however, can also be seen in the others. In *London Films*, for example, he describes the Parliament Houses on the Thames as "inevitably Gothic; they spring from the riverside as if they grew from the ground. . ." (p. 93). In *Seven English Cities* he concludes that cathedrals such as the one at Wells remind him of gardens. York Minster seems an "autumnal woodland" free of too much "architectural undergrowth" (p. 43).

The abundance of imagery of growth strongly intimates another dominant trait of English life—the natural and the man-made complement each other; in fact they often seem nearly synonymous. Nature has been assimilated, domesticated, and cultivated, but it has in turn stamped its character upon the Englishman. Howells feels that what has been stamped has merit. After his search for the elusive Marston Moor, he finds occasion to compare the "simple and gentle" English folk to Americans: "I went thinking that the difference was a difference between human nature long mellowed to its conditions, and human nature rasped on its edges and fretted by novel circumstances to a provisional harshness. I chose to fancy that unhuman nature sympathized with the English mood; in the sheep bleating from the pastures I heard the note of Wordsworth's verse; and by the sky, hung in its low blue with rough, dusky clouds, I was canopied as with a canvas of Constable's" (SEC, p. 72). Hawthorne advances a similar conclusion about the English: "They seem to have a great deal of earth and grimy dust clinging about them . . . and yet, though the individual Englishman is sometimes preternaturally disagreeable, an observer standing aloof has a sense of natural kindness towards them in the lump. They adhere closer to the original simplicity in which mankind was created than we ourselves do; they love, quarrel, laugh, cry, and turn their actual selves inside out with greater freedom than any class of Americans would consider decorous."[49] In England man has been fit for nature, and nature for man. In America growth implies change and uprooting, as Hawthorne suggests.[50] In England growth implies permanency.

According to F. O. Matthiessen, such writers of the American Renaissance as Emerson, Thoreau, and Whitman found the principle of organic form central to their conceptions of art. They generally accepted the notion that "just as the inner force of a phenomenon in nature determines its external structure, so the vitality of a poet's seminal idea or intuition determines its appropriate expression."[51] Howells appears to be interested in a somewhat similar principle, though he applies it to areas beyond art. It is possible that he became interested in the question of organic form after reading *English Traits,* in which Emerson cites a letter from Horatio Greenough setting forth his ideas about organic laws as they relate to architecture.[52] The explicit statements Howells makes about growth and the manner in which he allows primary images to "grow" in value strongly suggest an interest in a form which is more than mechanical or schematic.

Imagery of sound and movement often appears in conjunction with imagery of growth. Howells finds that so great and noisy a metropolis as London has surprisingly close ties to the natural world, a feature which James also notices.[53] Howells asks himself what characterizes London, and answers by saying: "it was endearingly nooky, cornery, curvy; with the enchantment of trees and flowers everywhere mixed with its civic turmoil, and the song birds heard through the staccato of cabs, and the muffled bellow of omnibuses" (*LF*, p. 135). This passage particularly illustrates the close proximity of primary images of growth, confusion, and sound. The natural and the artificial mingle and complement each other.

London traffic, which Howells sees as a characteristic feature of the city's vitality, creates "the effect of a single monstrous organism which writhes swiftly along the channel where it had run in the figure of a flood till you were tired of that metaphor" (*LF*, pp. 12-13). The "living" quality of London had prompted James to conclude that "so gorged an organism" imparts "the greatest sense of life."[54] In *English Traits* Emerson observed that Carlisle found London "the heart of the world," and remarkable only because of the "mass of human beings."[55] Perhaps it is inevitable that so vast and energetic a city should suggest a metaphor of bodily process to each writer.

Like Emerson and James, Howells sees London as a microcosm of a larger world. The city is, says Emerson, "the epitome of our times, and the Rome of today."[56] James sees it as "an epitome of the round world."[57] Howells approaches London-as-epitome much more indirectly. As a molecule in a vast organism, he is frequently borne along the current of its life in an omnibus. The omnibus, whose sound is characteristic, makes him feel "the insensate exultation of being a part of the largest thing of its kind in the world, or perhaps the universe" (*LF*, p. 13). He rides upon it in his often interrupted search of American origins. In it he forays into the sometimes impenetrable thicket of English history (*LF*, p. 218). He rumbles "earth-quakingly aloft" through the London haze which has the capability of transmuting him into the substance of a "dream made visible" (*LF*, pp. 9-10). The omnibus, as one of the more representative facts of English life, provides Howells with an excellent vantage point from which to observe the workings of the microcosm.

The omnibus, in turn, seems a microcosm in its own right. While it strikes Howells as "ugly, and bewilderingly painted over with the names of its destinations, and clad with signs of patent medicines and new plays and breakfast foods in every color but the colors of the rainbow" (*LF*, p. 48), he nevertheless sees it as a poetic fact of English life by its very commonness. It resembles the city in both size and character: it is the "most monumental fact of the scene," is "elephantine" in its gait (*LF*, p. 48), and has epic proportions (*LF*, p. 49). Impressive but grotesque, common but magnificent, the omnibus stirs Howells to humorous and hyperbolic statement. He finds in it a "barbaric majesty" (*LF*, p. 48); London's epic poet, should she ever have one, will sing the omnibus (*LF*, p. 49). Howells does not insist seriously that the omnibus be seen as emblematic. On the other hand, it is a most appropriate, democratic, and representative vehicle to choose for his London travels. From it the poetry of common life can best be glimpsed.

If the omnibus most adequately characterizes the common, the various, and the vital aspects of London life, houses and homes more generally characterize the whole of England. The individual homes Howells sees provide clues about the construction of a larger ancestral home. He often enough assumes imaginative ownership of English homes and property to indicate a more than incidental interest. In his treatment of homes he appears somewhat indebted to Hawthorne, as earlier suggested.

He also has two things in common with Henry VIII—an acquisitive nature and a liking for Tudor houses. The methods of acquisition differ, of course. To acquire a fine Tudor home Henry beheaded its owners, "a means of acquisition not so distasteful to him as to them" (*LF*, p. 157). Howells finds, as Henry must have found, that the Tudor house embodies a "high ideal of comfort" (*SEC*, p. 91) and he would gladly live in one of them. However, since such habitation is not feasible, he must devote his attention to possible connections between English character and English houses. He does this most explicitly in *Certain Delightful English Towns* when he comments on some family portraits: "They were of people who had a life in common with the house, wives and mothers and daughters, sons and husbands and fathers, married into it or born into it, and all receiving from it as much as they imparted to it, as if they were of one substance with it and it shared their consciousness that it was the home of their race. We have no like terms in America, and our generations, which are each separately housed, can only guess at the feeling for the place of their succession which the generations of such an English house must feel" (p. 100). Hawthorne likewise suggests his preference for a home which has grown out of a human heart and been reared by a man— a home which can be "his life-long residence, wherein to bring up his children, who are to inherit it as a home."[58] The final effect of a home built over the centuries is to impart "a sort of permanence to the intangible present."[59]

Howells differs from Hawthorne primarily in his emphasis on "shared consciousness" and reciprocating influence. The bond between house and man is a subtle one. A balance exists between them similar to that between man and nature in England. Cathedrals and churches are reflections of the natural world no more than houses are. All have grown out of the soil. When describing a country house, Howells discusses it as it reflects the closely knit conditions of existence in England: "Every such mansion is the centre of the evenly distributed civilization which he [the dweller] shares, and makes each part of England as tame, and keeps it as wild, as any other" (CDET, p. 101).

The "evenly distributed civilization" Howells sees embodied in the house did not altogether impress Emerson. He strongly states his preference for a less homogenous civilization. England is not wild enough, though it has energy enough: "A proof of the energy of the British people is the highly artificial construction of the whole fabric. The climate and geography, I said, were factitious, as if the hands of man had arranged the conditions. The same character pervades the whole kingdom."[60] Howells would argue, I suspect, that nature has equally arranged the conditions and that man, in his construction of the "artificial fabric," has often been prompted by nature. The homogeneity which he discovers in the people of England (CDET, p. 166) he also finds reflected in their homes.

Emerson asserts: "Domesticity is the taproot which enables the nation to branch wide and high. The motive and end of their trade and empire is to guard the independence and privacy of their homes."[61] Howells apparently agrees with him about the identity of the taproot, but he interprets "domesticity" quite differently. Rather than seeing it as a source of energy and power, he sees it as a further manifestation of the balance in English life. In the cathedral at Exeter he delights in the stoking of two "great iron stoves" which warm the edifice. These stoves "contribute in their humble way to that perfect balance of parts which is the most admired effect of its architectural symmetry" (CDET, p. 30). The stoking strikes him as "a bit of necessary housekeeping." It testifies as eloquently as anything to the characteristic "mingling of the poetical ideal and the practical real which has preserved them [the English] at every emergency" (CDET, p. 31). English houses are finely habitable because they reflect this mingling.

In corresponding fashion London's homelikeness "arises from its immense habitability" (LF, p. 223). The "home-keeping American mind" (CDET, p. 168) must painfully confess to the poverty of New World furnishings and admit that in contrast its own home seems temporary and provisional. It is hardly surprising that the American looks at English houses with such yearning and possessive eyes.

English houses certainly embody many of Howells' attitudes about continuity and permanence, yet he expresses his evident concern about these conditions in numerous other ways, both explicitly and implicitly. The degree to which the natural world suggests them to him has already been discussed, as has the indirect manner in which the images reflect his interest. On the whole, however, he presents his attitudes quite explicitly.

When at Exeter he remarks that in the presence of the cathedral he has a sense of the meaning of the "ages of faith." During those ages men were able to trust absolutely, believe richly, and hope fervently (CDET, p. 27). Their work demonstrated their faith. Howells knows that such faith and belief, and the necessary order which they imply, are not possible to his world. Yet, if faith and hope can no longer be guaranteed, even in England, tradition can perhaps insure some degree of significance, order, and coherence. Thus he often considers the matter of tradition, something not often taken account of by many Americans. The national tendency to disregard the past moved Hawthorne to observe, with some apprehension, that "our institutions may perish before we shall have discovered the most precious of the possibilities which they involve."[62]

Howells seems no less aware of the danger. And though he never comments so fully about the value of tradition to the artist as T. S. Eliot, much that Eliot says in "Tradition and Individual Talent" is implicit in the English travel books. When speaking about tradition and the historical sense, Eliot concludes: "the historical sense involves a perception not only of the pastness of the past, but of its presence; the historical sense compels a man to write not merely with his own generation in his bones, but with a feeling that the whole of the literature of Europe from Homer and within it the whole of the literature of his own country has simultaneous existence and composes a simultaneous order. The historical sense, which is a sense of the timeless as well as of the temporal together, is what makes a writer traditional. And it is at the same time what makes a writer most acutely conscious of his place in time, of his contemporaneity."[63] Howells certainly perceives the presence and the pastness of the past; he also concerns himself with the complex relationships between the timeless and the temporal. But he applies his perceptions in a more general way—he does not confine himself principally to the relationship between the artist and the literature of the past, and his area of investigation is more local. On the other hand, little doubt exists about the value he attaches to the historical sense. Though he often directs a humorous glance at the past, the humor serves primarily to suggest the complexity of his attitudes about time.

On occasion he treats the idea of time in a fanciful manner. When searching for the grave of George Fox, he discovers that he has two choices. He resolves the issue by suggesting that "in the process of time the two places may have become one and the same" (*LF*, p. 205). At more serious moments he acknowledges his desire to discover the timeless. At Oxford he observes that the spirit, when abroad, searches for a "common ground of actuality, achronic, ubiquitious [*sic*], where it may play with its fellow soul among the human interests which are eternally and everywhere the same" (*CDET*, p. 209).

Predictably enough, Howells maintains that he has no idea exactly what these eternal interests might be. Yet he does seek them. As he views cathedrals and churches, admires the natural beauty of the English countryside, or listens to the song of birds, the present sometimes dissolves into the past. At these times he hears, or nearly hears, the timeless voices speaking to a fellow soul. The moments when he is aware of the voices are fewer than he would wish, for in England "the living interests, ambitions, motives are so dense that you cannot penetrate them and consort quietly with the dead alone" (*LF*, p. 14). Yet the English books do reveal him listening for the voices of the dead more intently than before. He hears no intimations of personal immortality, but he discovers that perhaps tradition can preserve the essential features of the life of which man has been a part. The spirit can be given a form which will testify to its vitality in years to come.

When he visits St. Paul's, he finds impressive evidence of continuity and tradition. Here a list of bishops speaks to him "more eloquently of the infrangible continuity, the unbroken greatness of England" than portraits of "warriors and statesmen" (*LF*, p. 89). The bishops strike him so, apparently, because they have been more involved in transmitting "the original consciousness from age to age" (*CDET*, p. 85). This consciousness, he suggests, had its birth at the time of "the first articulate religions of the world" (*CDET*, p. 28).

Howells appears to appreciate the "unbroken continuity of ceremony, the essential unity of form" (*CDET*, p. 28) which he finds in the Anglican church; however, he does express some sympathy for those dissenters of the past who found form and ceremony oppressive to the individual soul (*CDET*, p. 28). He does not often endorse without qualification, and he can not be counted on to be wholly serious about continuity. At Bath the American discovers, to his chagrin, that in "the most actual and expensive of the arts," plumbing, the Romans have little to fear from American competition (*CDET*, p. 41). Continuity, it seems, applies even to plumbing.

One of the consequences of being a part of a tradition, Eliot maintains, is the sense of contemporaneity which it engenders. At Holy Trinity Goodramgate, an impressive Gothic church, Howells finds himself contemporaneous with the past: "The church did not look as if it felt itself a thousand years old, and perhaps it is not; but I was never in a place where I seemed so like a ghost of that antiquity. I had a sense of haunting it, in the inner twilight and the outer sunlight, where a tender wind was stirring the leaves of its embowering trees and scattering them on the graves of my eleventh century contemporaries" (*SEC*, p. 64). At another time he remarks that the "witchery" of poetry and romance in England has the effect of bringing "the tenth and twentieth centuries . . . bewilderingly together" (*CDET*, pp. 23-24). The mingling of the centuries, no less than the mingling of the natural and the artificial, testifies to the unity of experience. In becoming a ghost, Howells, in a sense, becomes what man has always been. When not a present ghost haunting the past, he observes the past haunting the present. He finds Bath charmingly haunted, and concludes: "the essential part of what has been anywhere seems to haunt the scene, and to become the immortal genius of the place" (*CDET*, p. 69).

Howells' discussions of the unity and continuity inherent in English life occasionally have apparent overtones of irony, humor, or hyperbole. But even so, the frequency with which he mentions or alludes to them indicates the extent of his involvement with ties which run "to the inmost and furthermost of our being" (*CDET*, p. 223). Ghosts testify to the ties and to the unity implicit in them.

In a different way death testifies to the same ties. Howells acknowledges the importance of death in any consideration of unity. Death, he realizes, is a significant part of existence which younger countries are more apt to deny than older ones (*LF*, p. 105). He amplifies his statement at York, where he views some graves of children: "Faith changes, but constant death remains the same, and life is not very different in any age, when it comes to the end. The Roman exiles who had come so far to hold my British ancestors in subjection to their alien rule seemed essentially not only of the same make as me, but the same civilization. Their votive altars and inscriptions to other

Gods expressed a human piety of like anxiety and helplessness with ours, and called to a like irresponsive sky" (*SEC*, p. 62).

Though death teaches, or should teach, something of the underlying unity of life, the source from which the unity springs is a mystery. Howells can only hint at it. He can no more state the meaning of the unity than Whitman can specify the meaning of the grass in "Song of Myself." Perhaps the "original consciousness" for which he searches is somewhere in the "depths of the ancestral past," which he hears echoed in the song of birds. Or perhaps "the scripturalized childhood of our race" can be found under the branches of a cedar of Lebanon tree (*CDET*, p. 19). The "consciousness" appears to have something to do with death, but just as often it has to do with the multitude of blossoms which attest to the regenerative force of life. It can not be discovered, though it can be sensed.

The English travel books are rich in discoveries and rewards for Howells' reader-companion, who has long ago discovered that when his guide insists on not being taken seriously, he probably should be. The travel books do contain a great deal of artistic merit. Howells' vision has widened and deepened, and his art reflects the expansion. In his handling of images and impressions he demonstrates a facility not evident in the Italian volumes. As much as ever he shows himself to be an accurate observer of society, as well as an acute critic of its failings. Though his volumes appear to be influenced by Emerson, Hawthorne, and James, they also demonstrate a highly original mind at work. They can be placed on the same shelf with *English Traits, Our Old Home,* and *English Hours,* without embarrassment.

The "obligations to consciousness" which England demanded of Howells have been met with as much success as is allowed travel writers who recognize their limitations and work within them. Howells has met them, not by becoming an expert about England's history and its present conditions, but by being true to the reality he sees, feels, and knows. In *London Films* he says of reality: "in proportion as we are ourselves real we love reality in other people, whether they are still alive or whether they died long ago" (p. 141). Perhaps in the proportion that Howells' readers sense the reality in themselves, they will discover their obligations to one who has explored the implications of the real so satisfactorily in these works.

NOTES

1. W. D. Howells, *London Films* (New York, 1906), p. 230. Subsequent references will be to this edition.

2. George Arms, "Howells' English Travel Books: Problems in Technique," *PMLA*, LXXXII (March 1967), 109. Arms observes that Howells recognized a "symbolic function in realism."

3. W. D. Howells, *Seven English Cities* (New York, 1909), p. 198. Subsequent references will be to this edition.

4. Maggie Brown Daniel, "A Study of William Dean Howells' Attitude Toward and Criticism of the English and Their Literature" (unpublished dissertation, University of Wisconsin, 1953), p. 95.

5. *Ibid.*, p. 100.

6. Edwin H. Cady, *The Realist at War* (Syracuse, N.Y., 1958), p. 250.

7. *Ibid.*

8. *Ibid.*, p. 252.

9. Arms, p. 105. I am indebted to Professor Arms for his suggestion that the influence of *English Traits* and *Our Old Home* on Howells' books might be investigated. Also, certain conclusions he draws about narrator identity, point of view, function of facts and of generalizations, and patterning of images have been especially valuable to me in my own investigations.

10. *Ibid.*, p. 106.

11. W. D. Howells, *Certain Delightful English Towns* (New York, 1906), p. 220. Subsequent references will be to this edition.

12. Nathaniel Hawthorne, *Our Old Home and English Note-Books*, in *The Works of Nathaniel Hawthorne*, ed. George Parsons Lathrop, 15 vols., Standard Library Edition, Vol. VII (Boston, 1891), p. 24.

13. *Ibid.*, p. 78.

14. *Ibid.*, p. 262.

15. Ralph Waldo Emerson, *English Traits* (Boston, 1856), p. 243.

16. *Ibid.*, p. 42.

17. *Ibid.*, p. 98.

18. *Ibid.*, p. 99.

19. *Ibid.*, p. 86.

20. *Ibid.*, p. 160.

21. *Ibid.*, p. 221.

22. *Ibid.*, p. 50.

23. Henry James, *English Hours,* ed. Alma Louise Lowe (London, 1960), p. 31.

24. Arms, p. 111.

25. *Ibid.,* p. 107. Arms explores in some detail the techniques Howells uses to handle facts and generalizations, as well as suggesting how these techniques relate to realistic practice.

26. Emerson, *English Traits,* p. 239.

27. Ralph Waldo Emerson, *Selections from Ralph Waldo Emerson: An Organic Anthology,* ed. Stephen Whicher, Riverside Edition (Boston, 1960), p. 90.

28. Emerson, *English Traits,* p. 34.

29. Arms, p. 108.

30. Hawthorne, pp. 77-78.

31. Arms, p. 111.

32. Hawthorne, p. 328.

33. Emerson, *English Traits,* p. 55.

34. *Ibid.,* p. 44.

35. James, *English Hours,* p. 8.

36. *Ibid.,* p. 2.

37. *Ibid.,* p. 43.

38. *Ibid.,* p. 24.

39. *Ibid.,* p. 30.

40. Leon Edel, ed. *The American Scene,* by Henry James (Bloomington, Ind., 1968), pp. xxv-xxvi.

41. *Ibid.,* p. ix.

42. James, *English Hours,* p. 14.

43. Emerson, *English Traits,* p. 40.

44. *Ibid.,* p. 287.

45. Hawthorne, p. 113.

46. *Ibid.,* p. 144.

47. *Ibid.,* p. 153.

48. *Ibid.,* p. 301. Howells appears to be responding either to Hawthorne or to a statement familiar to both of them when he says that the English, "if they did not build better than they knew, built better than we can" (*CDET,* p. 177).

49. Hawthorne, p. 267.

50. *Ibid.,* pp. 79-80.

51. F. O. Matthiessen, *American Renaissance* (New York, 1962), p. 134.

52. Emerson, *English Traits,* p. 12.

53. James, *English Hours,* p. 12.

54. *Ibid.,* p. 9.

55. Emerson, *English Traits,* p. 24.

56. *Ibid.*, p. 298.
57. James, *English Hours*, p. 8.
58. Hawthorne, p. 64.
59. *Ibid.*, p. 146.
60. Emerson, *English Traits*, p. 98.
61. *Ibid.*, p. 112.
62. Hawthorne, p. 147.
63. T. S. Eliot, "Tradition and Individual Talent," *The Great Critics: An Anthology of Literary Criticism*, eds. J. H. Smith and E. W. Parks, 3rd ed. (New York, 1961), p. 715.

5

EUROPE REVISITED:
VISION AND REAFFIRMATION

Roman Holidays (1908) and *Familiar Spanish Travels* (1913) are very different in their effects, but in both Howells demonstrates that he has lost none of his ability to transform the experience of travel into art. His eye for social and personal drama has never been sharper in a travel book than it is in *Roman Holidays,* and he has never sustained a fragile mood better than in *Familiar Spanish Travels.* At a time when he knows that many of his volumes have been forgotten,[1] he continues to battle quietly for realism in life and art. He reveals once more his deep belief that the material of common life has rich rewards for the artist who will look at it clearly and use methods which can reflect its significance. Many of the methods Howells uses are familiar, and the kind of material he considers has changed little, but he also makes new discoveries about techniques and materials. Those methods and attitudes which he reaffirms and the new directions which he takes will be the concern of this chapter.

Certainly *Roman Holidays* deserves a high rank among Howells' travel books, for it is finely crafted. Except for the rather slow chapters on visits to villas and tours to Tivoli and Frasca, he maintains interest remarkably well. The many roles he has assumed during his years as travel writer: realist, guide, humorist, critic, companion, social commentator, polite explorer—all are wonderfully balanced. In no other travel book does he reveal the facets of his mind and art so vividly and to such good effect.

For all its merits, *Roman Holidays* has been neglected. This neglect, in part, is attributable to the mistaken notion that Howells merely repeats the patterns established in his earlier work.[2] Woodress and Stiles suggest other faults. Though Woodress finds "the wisdom of age" in the work and further notes that Henry James and Charles Eliot Norton were impressed with Howells' "youthful zest for Italy," he judges that the book has "a certain prosaic quality."[3] Stiles states that it has "no particular element to make it remain in the mind."[4] Firkins, however, observes that its humor is irrepressible: "The amiability of the book is superlative; the reader could not wish it less—or more."[5]

The qualities of balance and proportion which Howells approves in some Italian art have much relevance to his own art. Both humor and balance bear looking into. Other aspects of the book which merit consideration are these: Howells' attitudes about art, architecture, and aesthetics; his continued interest in the drama of real life; his concern for social conditions and economic abuses; and his attitudes about history.

The realism toward which Howells unsuccessfully struggled in *Venetian Life* but which, for all his struggling, remained mostly anti-sentimentalism, has grown in complexity. In *Roman Holidays* he demonstrates how far he has gone down the "road to realism." As he has done in past volumes, he distinguishes between romance and realism frequently enough to remind the reader how basic the distinction is to his life and art. When he sees some realistic sculpture in the Campo Santo in Genoa, he confides to the reader that in his own "poor way" he has "striven for reality" (p. 31). He still strives for it, of course, and finds ample evidence of its value in most of his mild adventures. When he briefly leaves Gibraltar and goes two blocks into San Roque, Spain, he suggests that "a love of reality underlying all of my love of romance was satisfied in the impression left by that dusty, empty, silent street" (p. 24). A few pages later he concludes that some sculpture is "romanticistic" because of a "mixture of the real and the ideal" (p. 33). He has long preferred the real to the ideal, but has some momentary doubts about his preference. Half-seriously he wonders, "Is the true, then, better than the ideal, or is it only my grovelling spirit which prefers it?" (p. 140).

The question he asks is perhaps more rhetorical than interrogative. For better or worse his choice was made long ago. His "grovelling spirit" has found significance in the common, the small, and the trivial —a real achievement. In a letter of 1903 to Charles Eliot Norton, Howells admits that James may have been accurate in finding him deficient in "intellectual body." He uses the occasion of James' criticism to justify his method and material: "But I am not sorry for having wrought in common, crude material so much; that is the right American stuff; and perhaps hereafter, when my din is done, if any one is curious to know what that noise was, it will be found to have proceeded from a small insect which was scraping about on the surface of life and trying to get into its meaning for the sake of other insects larger or smaller."[6]

To embody his conception of the real, he primarily uses those techniques he used in *London Films* and *Certain Delightful English Towns*. He uses the impression less, but his attitudes about his audience, his conception of the role of the narrator, and his marginal interest in abundant facts have not changed. *Roman Holidays* does differ from the English books in its directness. Though Howells says at one point that no monument in Rome will be safe from his "indirect research" (p. 165), indirection counts for less than it did. He gladly takes what chance offers, but it offers less. And in Italy, for some reason, he does not find such a rich store of images and impressions as in England.

Roman Holidays differs from the earlier books on Italy in being more exclusively devoted to the drama of the present. At the Pincio, Howells records one of the slight dramatic episodes that he so enjoys. A young girl seems unsure of her suitor and suddenly runs from him "to the verge of the next fall of steps, possibly to show him how charmingly she was dressed, possibly to tempt him by her grace in flight to follow her madly. But he followed sanely and slowly, and she waited for him to come up, in a capricious quiet, as if she had not done anything or meant anything. That was all; but I am not hard to suit; and it was richly [sic] enough for me" (p. 108).

Such small sketches as these reveal that Howells has lost none of his sensitivity for quiet drama. He deftly portrays its slight gestures, mannerisms, and nuances. Often his dramatic episodes reveal characteristic features. Howells notices, for example, that a fellow traveler from Utah has "the true American spirit" when he insists on either going first class in Italy or going home (p. 67). On the other hand, some dramatic moments possess an irreducible particularity. When Howells motors about Rome, he rides with a woman of prodigious bulk. He finds himself "helpless against the recollection of this poor lady's wearing a thick motoring-veil which no curiosity could pierce, but which, when she lifted it, revealed a complexion of heated copper and a gray mustache such as nature vouchsafes to few women" (p. 171). Such "idle particulars" as this, he concludes, perversely cling to the memory, while more "ennobling facts" vanish absolutely.

Near the end of the volume he explicitly states the value he finds in the drama of travel. The occasion is the flight of a young girl from a musical comedy. Howells concludes: "It was one of those tacit, eventless dramas which in travel are always offering themselves to your witness. They begin in silence and go quietly to their unfinish, and leave you steeped in an interest which is life-long, whereas a story whose end you know soon perishes from your mind. Art has not yet learned the supreme lesson of life, which is never a tale that is told within the knowledge of the living" (p. 298). Howells' preference for incompleteness testifies to the value he finds in the living present; it also points to his greater interest in process and experience than in solutions and lessons.

The structural balance in *Roman Holidays* argues against "unfinish" as a primary virtue in the travel book. In an essay on Zola in 1902 Howells implied a preference for nonsymmetrical beauty—the beauty of the tree rather than the beauty of the temple. "Life," he suggests, "is no more symmetrical than a tree, and the effort of art to give it balance is to make it as false in effect as a tree clipped and trained to a certain shape."[7] But since Howells directs his criticism at what he considers the rigid formalities of French fiction, we can not conclude that he rejects the notion of balance. Balance which becomes the end of art or which calls attention to itself differs greatly from implicit balance. The balance in *Roman Holidays* is the second variety—it does not interfere with the sense of active experience which Howells wishes to render, and is instrumental in determining that effect.

Howells gives nearly equal space to the opening and closing sections of the book. The early and late chapters devoted to cities other than Rome neatly bracket the longer essay on Rome. The volume begins with Howells in Madeira rather than in Italy and ends appropriately enough with him out of Italy—in Monte Carlo (the dullest of imaginable Edens); Howells travels equally toward Rome and away from it. In several of the chapters on small cities he uses an envelope construction. He begins and closes the first chapter, "Up and Down Madeira," by calling attention to the spectacular and dramatic setting, one which far surpasses the "drop curtains" he has seen in theaters. In the second chapter, "Two Up-Town Blocks into Spain," he opens and closes with a discussion of his contrasting attitudes about the Rock of Gibraltar.

Howells relies a good deal on contrast to establish balance, or at least to suggest it. He contrasts, as we have seen, the real and the romantic, though he does not insist on differences with such fervor as he has. He also contrasts his intentions and the actualities of his experience. When in Rome he wishes to see the Baths of Caracalla first, but he sees them last (pp. 88-89). As he has done in the past, he characterizes himself as a polite, mild-mannered tourist, but he speaks, if anything, more vigorously of social inequities. He also effectively contrasts the old and the new—the Rome he has known and the Rome he now knows. Sometimes he contrasts nostalgia and present observation, careful qualifications and casual extravagance, and his social ideals and his concern with creature comforts.

The critic can do little more than suggest in a general way the large part humor plays in creating the effect in the volume. In *Venetian Life* and *Italian Journeys* humor served to reduce tensions between conflicting attitudes about Italy and America and to suggest a complex narrative perspective. In *Roman Holidays* it also reduces tensions, though the character of the tensions has changed. Howells accepts Europe's conditions with greater equanimity; his views are more inclusive and his treatment more judicious. The tensions are now more personal and social than national. They primarily exist between the unequal social conditions of the world he sees and the world of social equality he has dreamed of, and between his young spirit and his old body.

Sometimes the term "humor" fails to give an adequate sense of the unique quality of Howells' statement. "Wit" seems a preferable word, but "wit" with some of the meanings it had in the eighteenth century: the ability to perceive connections, to explore relationships, and to come to insights about moral values. This wit becomes particularly evident when Howells treats society's excesses and frailties. Yet his humor reflects a cheerful disposition more than anything else. Though he sometimes assumes a gay pose to keep the reader from disturbing thoughts about the past's cruelties (p. 91), he frequently seems cheerful for his own sake. When he says he would be pleased to see a suicide at Monte Carlo (p. 284) or to be a "German student of theology" if he could wear a colorful costume (p. 126), he is hardly serious.

Howells evidently delights as much as ever in paradox, hyperbole, and extravagant personification. He sees a rainbow with a "stout and athletic" leg (p. 2) and a sunset of "watermelon red" (p. 46). Some catacombs—"among the cheerfulest of all the catacombs"—win his praise (p. 234), while a "cowering stove" in Leghorn loses its stovepipe in a vast, arctic room and wins his censure (pp. 243-44). At Pisa he gazes at some "unforgettable, forgotten" paintings by Andrea del Sarto (p. 261). Nevertheless, Howells' humor knows its place. It does not intrude, but it does not often fail to surprise and delight.

The humorous iconoclasm and the brash irreverence of *Venetian Life* and *Italian Journeys* have yielded to a more consistent ironic method. But Howells evidently felt that in *Roman Holidays* he had once more found "the touch which had brought him acclaim as a young man."[8] When he notes that a bronze Marcus Aurelius majestically bestrides a bronze charger, "an extremely fat one" (p. 115), he is near the spirit of his early work; he is also near when he observes that in the cathedral in Naples he sees "everything but the blood of St. Jannarius, perhaps because it was not then in the act of liquefying" (p. 46). Though his irreverence recalls old attitudes, it more frequently calls attention to the foibles and stupidities of *man* than to the deficiencies of Italians and Italian civilization. Howells' ready allegiance to American morals and habits has vanished. In the years since his first trip to Venice he has learned that all men are essentially the same—even in their foolishness.

The humor in *Venetian Life* often had its origin in differences between conventional treatments of scenes and objects of interest and Howells' treatment of these. His business was primarily to correct false notions through humorous undercutting. In *Roman Holidays* the conventions of sentiment and rhapsody are so far in the past that they do not even merit much ridicule. Byron has fallen, and Howells himself becomes the primary obstacle to proper appreciation. He knows that his own memory or experience, for better or worse, stands between him and the object or scene he looks at. The Rock of Gibraltar, an impressive sight, is less than it might be because it resembles "the trade-mark of the Prudential Insurance Company"; Howells can not help thinking that the rock has been plagiarized (p. 14).

More than in the other Italian books Howells stresses the incongruity inherent in his position, the conflict between what he is and what he ideally ought to be. His relative wealth embarrasses him, so from time to time he reminds his reader of the guilt proper to one of his station. At least he has the right sympathies. He playfully and ironically admits to a "snobbish soul" (p. 186) and complains that he sees no persons of fashion.

His "snobbish soul" often consorts with strikers, beggars, grocery men, cab drivers. He mentions his acts of charity often—some might say too often—but less from pride in his benevolence than from guilt. Fortunately, his admissions of charity have a humorous or critical edge to them. When he gives, he becomes something less than blessed, as he eloquently proves in a memorable passage. He indignantly discusses beggary and ruefully considers the complexities involved in the charitable act:

> I am not sure that there are even more beggars in Naples than in New York, though I will own that I kept no count. In both cities beggary is common enough, and I am not noting it with disfavor in either, for it is one of my heresies that comfort should be constantly reminded of misery by the sight of it—comfort is so neglectful. Besides, in Italy charity costs so little; a cent of our money pays a man for the loss of a leg or an arm; two cents is the compensation for total blindness; a sick mother with a brood of starving children is richly rewarded for her pains with a nickel worth four cents. Organized charity is not absent in the midst of such volunteers of poverty; one day, when we thought we had passed the last outpost of want in our drive, two Sisters of Charity suddenly appeared with out-stretched tin cups. Our driver did not imagine our inexhaustible benevolence; he drove on, and before we could bring him to a halt the Sisters of Charity ran us down, their black robes flying abroad and their sweet faces flushed with the pursuit. Upon the whole it was very humiliating; we could have wished to offer excuses and regrets; but our silver seemed enough, and the gentle sisters fell back when we had given it. (p. 51)

The dramatic episode has a grim sort of humor because of its studied casualness and because of the gentle sisters' energetic pursuit and their evident satisfaction in having overtaken the humble givers. More than anything the passage suggests how far Howells has come since the time of *Venetian Life*. There he could make use of the picturesqueness of poverty. Now he reacts with fierce indignation to the notion that physical disability and hunger have their appropriate scale of prices.

To make his points, Howells does not hesitate to give his reader some stark fact and then intensify its effect by implicitly contrasting it to a politer one. He suggests in Madeira that some beggars "with fingers reduced to their last joints" might be lepers, but does not insist upon it (p. 7). A paragraph later, with the memory of the beggars still fresh, he mentions the famine of himself and his companions; they have not eaten for three hours, "which was long for saloon passengers" (p. 8). The world, he later observes, has not yet become as "sternly collectivist" as he would have it (p. 287). Until it becomes so he must guiltily act in the drama of social inequality. What he gives can not be enough, and he finds the realization disquieting.

Class conflict also has its lighter side. The sight of capitalists struggling with their luggage because of a strike leads Howells to observe with ironic sadness: "they were all laden according to their strength, and people who had never done a stroke of work in their lives were actually carrying their own hand-bags, rugs, and umbrella-cases. It was terrible" (p. 162). When Howells sees a shad swimming about in an aquarium, he observes that the fish has a "surly dignity becoming to people in better society than others" (pp. 53-54). The fish, perversely enough, resembles George Washington.

The wealthy American is often the target of Howells' criticism. For those American millionaires who belong to the best society Howells advances a modest proposal. They can insure themselves some sort of immortality and also do America inestimable service by fostering the art of grave portraiture. After Howells sees such portraits in Genoa he concludes: "To the American who views them and remembers that we have now so much money that some of us do not know what to do with it, they will suggest that our millionaires have an unrivalled opportunity of immortality. . . . There is hardly a town of ten thousand inhabitants where there are not men who could easily afford to give a hundred thousand dollars, or fifty, or twenty to their native or adoptive place and so enter upon a new life in bronze or marble" (p. 281).

Americans come in for a good share of criticism, and Howells does not slight other nationalities. But he directs more of his criticism at the species than at particular civilizations. He hopes, "for the credit of our species," that a very swift one-legged beggar lost his leg in war, as he romantically should have (p. 107). In Rome he appreciates the soldiers he sees because he finds "comparatively few of them" (p. 125), and at a more serious time complains because there are "more military memories in the world than is good for it" (p. 18). The world evidently needs more improvements and fewer war glories or nationalistic sentiments. Howells prefers to have Rome less picturesque and more free of typhoid (p. 80). If the new electric light glaring in the dungeon where St. Peter was held does not strike him as the most necessary of improvements (p. 135), he finds much else in New Rome to approve. The Rome which he found "hideous" in *Italian Journeys* now provides him great joy. And perhaps even forty years ago it was not so hideous as he suggested; he writes to Charles Eliot Norton that he and his wife are renewing with Rome the acquaintance they had "so intimately, so rather passionately when we were twenty-seven instead of seventy."[9]

Firkins accurately attributes the excellence of *Roman Holidays* to Howells' treatment of "weighty general topics—New Rome, the two-day strike, the present Italian government—which should compact and solidify a work of travel."[10] Howells frequently treats such topics humorously, but he also speaks seriously of them. He terms the two days' strike by "far the most impresssive experience of our Roman winter; in some sort it was the most impressive experience of my life, for I beheld in it a reduced and imperfect image of what labor could do if it universally chose to do nothing" (p. 159). Yet he can not approve the violence which accompanies the strike. He reports details about the violence with a calm which suggests his dismay. "Four persons," he says, "were killed, with the usual proportion of innocent spectators" (p. 160). In none of the other travel books has Howells' social conscience been more active than it now is, and in no other does he speak so freely or imply so much of his social idealism. At times he seems a Mr. Homos in disguise—though he advocates less comprehensive programs than the Altrurian traveler does.

When Howells criticized Europe's past, in *Venetian Life* and *Italian*

Journeys, he showed his strong moral bias. This bias implied not only that history was understandable, but that he understood it. By the time of *Roman Holidays* he does not pretend to understand it. His search through the years for history's uses and meanings has turned up few meanings and fewer uses. Now he finds history "a very baffling study, and one may be well content to know little or nothing about it" (p. 47). It is baffling in spite of increased knowledge of it—it has something of the nature of an abyss. When Howells visits the Coliseum and sees where senseless slaughters have occurred, he concludes: "One must make light of such things or sink under them" (p. 91). In *Tuscan Cities* he could not make light of them, and he nearly sank. But now his sense of the immediate scene and the revelations of the present moment keep him afloat.

Though history often baffles Howells, at times it is merely irrelevant. In the Forum he feels the great "pathos of human grief" when he sees the remains of a child. The sight leads him to conclude that "history in the presence of such world-old atomies seemed an infant babbling of yesterday" (p. 97). In *London Films* and *Certain Delightful English Towns* Howells demonstrated his interest in going beyond history to find the source of unity and continuity in civilization. He shows less interest in either history or the source by the time of *Roman Holidays*. "It is better," he says, "to have too little past, as we [Americans] have than too much, as they [Italians] have" (p. 28). Too much past evidently proves an obstacle to understanding the necessities of the present. Howells devotes a chapter of *Roman Holidays* to his attempt to be honest about antiquity, and he is most honest when he admits that he can not take it very seriously.

Baroque art still offends him, and he spiritedly criticizes it. He does not respond to its vigor, and evidently he can not understand the vision or imagination which prompted its creation. In St. Peter's he claims that baroque saints and popes "swagger in their niches or over their tombs in an excess of decadent taste for which the most bigoted agnostic, however Protestant he may be, must generously grieve" (p. 130). Typically enough, however, when he grieves for excess one day, he inclines toward tolerance on the day following (p. 132). His moral absolutes more often than not turn out to be provisional conclusions.

Sometimes he can not specify the particular quality in art which appeals to him. About the antique columns of the Temple of Neptune, for example, he can say little: "I could not say why their poor, defaced, immortal grandeur should have always so affected me, I do not know that my veneration was due it more than many other fragments of the past; but no arch or pillar of them all seems so impressive, so pathetic" (p. 115). When Howells suggests why a particular work appeals to him, he speaks in general and subjective terms. His dismay over what he considers to be the excessive statement and rampant individualism in baroque art (p. 120) prompts his preference for the "serenity and sanity" he finds in Greek art (p. 183). At another point he allows that Canova is "tame," but also finds him wonderfully "sane." He prefers Canova to Michelangelo because Canova's sculpture has a "truth of repose" in it (p. 146). Two other qualities which Howells admires, but only briefly mentions, are relation and proportion. After he sees what he terms a "crazy agglomeration" of "warring forms" in the Forum, he advocates the need for "collective beauty" (p. 94). Individual forms must contribute to the effect of the whole.

As he has in past volumes, Howells finds art criticism or art history a hindrance to aesthetic experience. He maintains that tolerance, not knowledge, "accounts for a good deal of the appreciation and even the criticism of works of art" (p. 154). Criticism is fickle, "especially in its final judgments" (p. 174), and the viewer would do well to respond as honestly as possible to what he sees. If he does so, he may unexpectedly discover, as Howells does when he sees some work of Veronese, that he may have "always had some little sense of art" (p. 146). Of course Howells will not admit to having the sense for more than a moment or two. Perhaps it is, after all, "only a literary sense of art" (p. 146).

A reader may have some misgivings about the adequacy of Howells' response to art. On the whole, however, he should have few misgivings about the artistry evident in *Roman Holidays*. Howells vividly demonstrates in this last Italian book that he has lost none of his love for "the home of human nature." Though he will write a travel sketch of San Remo in 1920,[11] the year of his death, he effectively closes his account with Italy in *Roman Holidays*. Certainly it is a fitting climax to his long and rewarding involvement with Italy.

Familiar Spanish Travels, Howells' last major travel book, possesses charm in abundance, as several critics have noted. The mood of nostalgia in the book makes it, as Firkins observes, "foremost in attractiveness."[12] But it also has some shortcomings, which the critic inclines to forgive. Because of its nostalgia, it seems to ask gentle handling. In 1910 Howells had lost his wife, Elinor, and his friends, Mark Twain and Larkin Mead. He was, Cady concludes, "doomed to make the stoical best, in a 'cheerful despair,' of a decade of exile to the far-away land of old age."[13] Howells acknowledges that he knows the quality of such cheer. He finds it present when he observes the Spanish visiting cemeteries, in memory of their dead. In many of the mourners he sees "a sort of cheerfulness which bereavement sometimes knows."[14] In *Familiar Spanish Travels* the faraway land of old age has much in common with the faraway land of youth.

His sense of loss probably contributes to his wistful recollection of those times in his boyhood when he committed his imagination to adventures in Spain. Now at seventy-four he travels in Spain for the first time and acknowledges that his record must be "more or less autobiographical" (p. 2). Throughout his travels he often refers to his youthful impressions and dreams of Spain, and young boys richly populate his pages. These boys serve a kind of formal requirement, inasmuch as they provide Howells a means of contrasting age and youth. Yet they also suggest his desire to recapture at least as much of his youth as his always ironic perspectives will allow him.

Howells creates unity of effect in the volume primarily through contrast. The contrast between youth and age is central, and most other contrasts contribute to the complexity of this basic one. Howells also creates order by utilizing motifs and allusions to literary figures. More than in other volumes, he makes the literary pilgrimage an important ingredient in his design. Two other aspects of the book worth consideration are his descriptions of landscape and his use of drama and dramatic devices to impart his sense of the human comedy he sees in Spain—a comedy in which he often plays the lead.

Familiar Spanish Travels has no very grievous faults, but they are apt to irritate Howells' younger readers. The attention he pays to unpleasant smells, insufficient heating, and poor accommodations may be explained as the inevitable concerns of an aged traveler whose body functions less efficiently than it once did. Nevertheless, his frequent references to the trivia of travel do become tedious at times, and one may justly complain that they detract from the effect.

Howells also allows himself an ease of generalization not found in previous books, and he often generalizes from fewer facts. When he admits basing a conjecture on narrow grounds (p. 24), he speaks more truly than one would wish. Grounds are suspiciously narrow when he describes a dancer who has "the square-jawed, high-cheek-boned face of the lower class Spaniard" (p. 237). Earlier in Valladolid he attributed to men of high cheekbones a middle-class position (p. 71). Spanish women, he suggests, surpass their mates in being "handsomer and better dressed." They possess an altogether "finer social and intellectual quality" (p. 70). Such generalizations as these suggest that Howells has not looked deeply into the structure of Spanish society. Stiles rightly judges that in *Familiar Spanish Travels* Howells demonstrates less interest in "social institutions and social relationships."[15]

Fortunately, the virtues of the volume outweigh its deficiencies. A notable virtue is Howells' treatment of the Spanish landscape. The landscape he now sees has little in common with the imaginative vistas of his youth. In Basque country he notes the disparity:

I must own that the Spain I was now for the first time seeing was so little like the Spain of my boyish vision that I never once recurred to it. That was a Spain of cork trees, of groves by the green margins of mountain brooks, of habitable hills, where shepherds might feed their flocks and mad lovers and maids forlorn might wander and maunder; and here were fields of corn and apple orchards and vineyards reddening and yellowing up to the

door of those comfortable farmhouses, with nowhere the sign
of a Christian cavalier or a turbaned Infidel. As a man I could
not help liking what I saw, but I could also grieve for the boy
who would have been so disappointed if he had come to the
Basque provinces of Spain when he was from ten to fifteen years
old, instead of seventy-four. (pp. 11-12)

The lush landscapes of the boy contrast sharply with the desolate
scenes the old man sees throughout Spain. Though Howells treats the
boy's vision with some irony, he obviously can not altogether forget the
vision—nor completely forgive his young self for having it.

Some of the most striking passages in *Familiar Spanish Travels* are
descriptions of desolate countryside. A memorable example, worth
citing at length, is his description of the area between Valladolid and
Madrid:

It was . . . as if we were crossing the face of some prodigious
rapid, whose surges were the measureless granite boulders toss-
ing everywhere in masses from the size of a man's fist to the size of
a house. In a wild chaos they wallowed against one another, the
greater bearing on their tops or between them on their shoulders
smaller regular or irregular masses of the same gray stone.
Everywhere among their awful shallows grew gray live-oaks, and
in among the rocks and trees spread tufts of gray shrub. Suddenly over the frenzy of this mad world, a storm of cold rain
broke whirling, and cold gray mists drove, blinding the windows
and chilling us where we sat within. From time to time the
storm lifted and showed again this vision of nature hoary as if with
immemorial eld; if at times we seemed to have run away from it
again it closed upon us and held us captive in its desolation.
(p. 83)

Throughout the passage Howells echoes, in his prose rhythms and
diction, the movement and disorder suggested by the "prodigious
rapid" of the first sentence; the strong verbs and participles, the rush-
ing sounds, and the irregular rhythm ("in a wild chaos they wallowed

against one another") vividly impart a sense of rapid movement and intolerable disorder.

When Howells speaks of the "poor scruples of moderation" he abides by in his descriptions of landscapes, he does not specify the nature of his scruples. However, he suggests them in his method: he will not use lush and standard diction; he will describe what he sees rather than what he knows the reader has seen before; he will be selective rather than graphic in his use of detail; and he will stand by his impressions.

During his Spanish travels Howells gives freer rein to his fancy than he has in past journeys. As a consequence, the reader often has a sense of seeing what might be termed "interior perspectives"—that is, Howells impresses his fancy and memory on the material he sees, fleshes out a scene with his imagination, and emphasizes the subjective response. We see a humorous example of this tendency when, as he tours the countryside around Toledo, he sees a "lordly black pig." It so strikes his fancy that he discusses its significance in mock heroic terms: "His statuesque pose was of a fine hauteur, and a more imaginative tourist than I might have fancied him lost in a dream of the past, piercing beyond the time of the Iberian autochtons [sic] to those prehistoric ages 'when wild in woods the noble savage ran,' pursuing or pursued by his tusked and bristled ancestor, and then slowly reverting through the different invasions and civilizations to that signal moment when, after three hundred Moslem years, Toledo became Christian again forever, and pork resumed its primacy at the table. Dark, mysterious, fierce, the proud pig stood, a figure made for sculpture" (pp. 142-43).

Evidently pigs, like authors, also dream of the past, and in *Familiar Spanish Travels* pigs are made the most romantic objects in all of Spain. Howells applies the romantic vision and language of the boy in him to the most incongruous object possible, and the effect is delightful. The pigs Howells introduces to the reader are much more imaginative than real, but one gladly meets them. Howells' pigs normally serve to qualify or undercut romantic notions, but on occasion they have a more pedestrian function. In Burgos he sees some wineskins, made from pigskins, and he rejoices in his realization of "how Spanish, how literary, how picturesque, how romantic" the wineskins are (p. 43). The sight brings back memories of his boyhood as "nothing else had yet" (p. 43). The boy found romance in wineskins; the old man finds the romance of real life in the "low industry" of preparing pigskins.

Howells consistently contrasts the romance of his youth to the realism of his maturity. Often he does so through literary allusions. Don Quixote and Sancho Panza, for example, have some things in common with the boy and the old man. Quixote's idealism and romantic notions offer Howells some ready correspondences with his youth. In his age and skepticism he serves as a kind of Sancho Panza to the young Howells who travels with him. Sancho Panza warns and then implores the gallant Quixote not to enter into combat with the windmills (p. 169). The boy and the old man always accuse each other; the boy finds the old man a dodderer while the old man finds the boy a dreamer (p. 6).

Yet just as the squire and his knight are necessary to each other, so are the old and young Howells—at least in *Familiar Spanish Travels*. The "chord of autobiography" which Howells strikes testifies to a "harmony between the boy and the old man" (p. 6), and this in turn suggests a harmony of vision. One must have seen, at some time, a "knight skipping on the rocks in a single garment" (p. 171) before he can determine the value of or reason for his own conduct. Basic to Howells' conception of the real is his knowledge of the part the incongruous and absurd play in an "unbalanced world" (p. 111).

Howells has learned through experience that "man born of woman is hungry" and that man must abandon the "winged steed of dreaming" if he is to appease "unflagging appetite" (p. 127). Yet the dream has served to whet the appetite for life; illusion is necessary to actuality, opposition to unity. The boy who planned to write of Cervantes' life and who dreamed of Spain as fair and noble has grown up; he now finds the reality of "squalid children" and feels the horror of seeing the "body of a drowned man on the sand, poorly clothed in a workman's dress, and with his poor, dead clay-white hands stretched out from him on the sand, and his gray face showing to the sky" (p. 76).

The contrast of youthful romance and mature realism bears upon the attitudes about literature and life which Howells expresses. He assures the reader that "literature and its associations, no matter from how lowly suggestion, must always be first for me" (p. 44). His own work, however, belies the assertion. He does allude to literary figures on numerous occasions, but the allusions serve primarily to illustrate the changes which have occurred in his perspectives about life. He finds, for example, that the actual country where Don Quixote lived hardly resembles "the country I had read out of his history in my boyhood" (p. 168). He then notices that "one carries out of one's reading an image which one has carried into it" (p. 168). When he visits the Alhambra, made famous by Washington Irving, he discovers that it has none of the "marble and gold" he had imagined it as having (p. 277). And in Valladolid, where Cervantes once lived, the unhappy pilgrim smells a "noisome stench" coming from Cervantes' old house (p. 73).

One can not doubt the experience of a "stench," but one can doubt that history leads to an understanding of experience. "History itself is often of two minds about the facts, or the truth from them" (p. 226), Howells reports, and because it is of two minds, he prefers drama. Drama, at least, seems better able to illustrate the actualities of experience. He recalls that he has been a "lifelong lover of the drama" (p. 294). In Ohio, when a boy, he knew the work of Moratin, "the historian of the Spanish drama" (p. 117); he once translated a "ridiculously romantic" play by Estebanez (p. 95).

The unromantic drama of Goldoni has been a major influence on his own art, and he gratefully acknowledges the influence. He concludes, at one point, that a quarrel he sees was "perfectly like a scene of Goldoni and like many a passage of real life" (p. 242). The passages of real life which Howells dramatizes have not changed appreciably in fifty years. Howells plays a more active role in these passages than in the past, a fact attributable to the incidence of autobiography in the book.

Howells knows that his adventures are slight, but they, at least, are his. Were they fraught with danger, his readers, who have long survived on mild adventure, would not admit them. Unlike Hemingway, who finds profound drama in the bull ring, Howells hopes to find his drama in the crowd attending the bull fight (p. 92). When describing his trip from Ronda to Gibraltar, he ironically suggests that for once "the journey was without those incidents which have so often rendered these pages thrilling" (p. 309). Immediately after admitting the deficiency, however, he records one of the most pleasant dramatic incidents in the volume. He discovers that he must travel first class with some domestics who have only third-class tickets; unfortunately, he must also travel with their dog, who has no ticket at all and who curls up dangerously near his ankle. His sense of his danger leads him to observe that "in traveling first class one must draw the line at dogs" (p. 310).

Throughout his Spanish travels Howells finds himself acting out brief comedies of manners with dogs, guides, porters, drivers, hotel managers, or fellow tourists. The reader, after he has shared Howells' dismay and delight in his slight adventures, wishes to say, as Howells does: "After this passage of real life it was not easy to sink again to the level of art . . ." (p. 67).

To sink to something as fine as Howells' art is to sink hardly at all. The light drama he records in Spain keeps a spirit afloat, and even warm. The warmth of the book, however, is the warmth of Indian Summer. When one thinks of the old man traveling about with an illusory boy, it is hard not to feel some sadness. One nearly hears Howells saying, as the speaker does in Emily Dickinson's poem, "These are the days when Birds come back:" "Oh Sacrament of summer days,/ Oh last communion in the Haze—/ Permit a child to Join."[16]

Near the end of *Familiar Spanish Travels* Howells appears to have overtaken the "fugitive summer" (p. 15) he has long pursued, and he vividly describes the experience: "after we had left a mountain valley where the mist hung grayest and chillest, we suddenly burst into a region of mellow fruitfulness, where the haze was all luminous, and where the oranges hung gold and green upon the trees, and the women brought peaches and apples to the train. The towns seemed to welcome us southward and the woods we knew instantly to be of cork trees, with Don Quixote and Sancho Panza under their branches everywhere we chose to look" (p. 306). But winter can not be far behind, and with reluctance the reader says of this Indian Summer, as Dickinson said of the one she knew, "Almost thy plausibility/ Induces my belief."[17] It is a touching moment when Howells takes leave of the last of the many boys he has met and says to us: "To this hour I do not know how we ever brought ourselves to part with him" (p. 306). The reader who parts with *Familiar Spanish Travels* does so with the same sense of reluctance.

Roman Holidays and *Familiar Spanish Travels* differ in many ways. The Italian book contains an enviable wit, a wealth of shrewd social commentary, and a fine vigor of expression. In execution it is the equal of *London Films*. Howells' account of his Spanish travels is more obviously subjective. Material counts for less than it has previously, and fancy and mood count for more. *Familiar Spanish Travels* is a more leisurely book, and Howells does not criticize as sharply as he has done. In spite of these differences, however, a consistent purpose of realism can be seen in both. Howells reaffirms his belief in the principles of realism which have been necessary to his life and art. He values what his art exemplifies: moderation, proportion, grace of expression, humor, and truthful treatment of character, scene, and experience.

NOTES

1. W. D. Howells, *Roman Holidays and Others* (New York, 1908), p. 187. Subsequent references will be to this edition.

2. Both Woodress and Wright maintain that in *Roman Holidays* Howells relies on past patterns. Woodress finds a "marked similarity both in plan and execution" with *Italian Journeys* (p. 195), and Wright states that the later books follow the "general pattern" established by the earlier ones (p. 178).

3. Woodress, pp. 195-96.

4. Stiles, p. 61.

5. Firkins, p. 56.

6. W. D. Howells, *Life in Letters*, II, 173.

7. W. D. Howells, *William Dean Howells: Representative Selections*, eds. Rudolf and Clara Marburg Kirk, Revised Edition (New York, 1961), p. 374.

8. Woodress, pp. 194-95.

9. *Life in Letters*, II, 250.

10. Firkins, p. 56.

11. Woodress, p. 193.

12. Firkins, p. 56.

13. Cady, *The Realist at War*, p. 254.

14. W. D. Howells, *Familiar Spanish Travels* (New York, 1913), p. 253. Subsequent references will be to this edition.

15. Stiles, p. 87.

16. Emily Dickinson, *The Complete Poems of Emily Dickinson*, ed. Thomas H. Johnson (Boston, 1960), p. 61.

17. *Ibid.*

6

CONCLUSIONS

Howells' travel accounts do not presume to be immortal, but they deserve consideration because of their American flavor and their artistry. A study of Howells' work is the study of a developing artist and his personal and social conscience. The most significant of Howells' critical positions relates to vision: The new and the exotic have no inherent significance; the significance lies in the eye, for the eye which sees clearly can discover freshness in the most common material. Because the eye acts upon the world it sees, any estimate of that world will depend on the perspective of the viewer. When Howells reviews Arnold Bennett's *Your United States* in 1913, he reaffirms his belief in the necessity for clear and honest vision. Through a dialogue between the Easy Chair, a First Citizen, and a Second Citizen, Howells reveals his belief. The First Citizen observes that Bennett has found "the poetry, the romance he came for."[1] What Bennett came for, the Citizen continues, is "the Kiplingesque heroic ballad, the dingdong, the hammer-and-tongs epic, the mighty and lusty music of our tremendous civilization, and he found that. He beheld the colossal people 'getting results' whom he expected to see, and he found the phrase ready to greet his apt and instant sense which seized upon it so joyfully."[2] The First Citizen praises Bennett ironically. Unlike Howells, Bennett seeks evidence of what he knows, and he sees what he expects to see. Though Bennett's book may be "brilliantly interesting,"[3] as the Easy Chair suggests, the American who thought that his country had some faults is embarrassed by the excessive praise of "the kindest of our critics."[4]

Howells knows that the kindest and most salutary critic honestly reports what he finds, feels, and sees. Certainly a primary aim of Howells was to record his discoveries and his feelings with fidelity. In his critical reviews he expresses admiration for those writers who write honestly of their experience. However, he places equal value on artistry, for he realizes that techniques have moral consequences. His books show increasing respect for the relation of technique to honesty. Howells discovered in *Tuscan Cities* that the methods he had used to record the reality of travel in *Venetian Life* and *Italian Journeys* no longer suited his vision. In his later books, from *London Films* through *Familiar Spanish Travels,* he experiments with techniques of indirection to suggest "reality" more effectively. To create his effects he turns to image clusters, dramatic encounters, and impressions.

Of the ideas Howells expresses in his reviews, those treating point of view, selectivity of detail, and generalization have continuing relevance to his own work. In these reviews Howells several times states that the writer who leaves nothing out often puts less in than he might; that if a writer assumes no consistent attitude about the roles he assigns his narrator, sharp contrasts in tone may result; and that the relationship between facts and generalizations may often be tenuous. Howells prefers to generalize from experience and sees his responses as those of a typical traveler. He consistently refuses to judge absolutely what he sees, for circumstance often modifies truth. Therefore, he utilizes techniques which can handle the truths of the moment. He voices tentative generalizations and argues against finality. He renders impressions, records fragments, and uses images in an attempt to come as close to the reality of the present as possible. Often, when he generalizes, he has near at hand a concrete fact. In the absence of absolute values or final truths he approaches reality pragmatically.

Because of his active involvement with the present, Howells experiences difficulty in coming to terms with the past. Yet he deals with it more seriously than some critics credit him with doing. In *Venetian Life* and *Italian Journeys* he expresses dismay at the cruelties of the past, but still feels that the past must be considered. In *Tuscan Cities* he impresses the present upon the past. By becoming contemporaneous with the past, he attempts to re-humanize it; he also expects it to yield useful moral conclusions. He approaches history more indirectly and more successfully in *London Films, Certain Delightful English Towns,* and *Seven English Cities.* His search for American historical origins becomes a search for a timeless reality, and in the emblems of English history he finds clues to this reality. When he writes *Roman Holidays* and *Familiar Spanish Travels,* he concludes that he has found the study of the past baffling, and, because it often is baffling or deceptive, and occasionally because it is irrelevant, the traveler had best take his chances with the present. Howells hardly advances these late conclusions about the past facilely, for behind them stand more than fifty years of writing and reading history and nearly seventy of experiencing it.

Howells' experience with the visual arts has also been long, and upon this experience he bases his belief that art should be relevant to life. Art history and art criticism, he feels, often stand between the viewer and his appreciation, and, because language can not adequately suggest the aesthetic qualities which the viewer responds to, descriptions of statues and paintings have little value. Because he does not speak as an authority, his judgments about particular works of art are less important than his belief that pictures and sculpture must be individually and repeatedly experienced if one is to come to understand and appreciate them.

A man standing dully before the canvas of a master, a janitor firing a furnace in the cathedral, or two sisters of charity pursuing reluctant capitalists—these figures, and hundreds more grace Howells' pages and testify to his abiding interest in the human scene. This interest seems most likely to insure the value of his work. Indeed, many of his techniques seem shaped to reveal the human element in the sharpest and truest light possible. While *Venetian Life* and *Italian Journeys* have the merits of youthful irreverence, vigor, and iconoclasm, they do show Howells' tendency to sacrifice his characters to the picturesque or the sentimental. His humane sympathies are stronger by the time of *Tuscan Cities,* though his view of man is darker than it was in the 1860's. The volumes written after the turn of the century demonstrate his continued delight in the variety and vitality of human life. His view of man is sympathetic but unromantic and critical, and he criticizes the failings of his fellows at the same time he admits his kinship with them.

The numerous dramatic encounters which Howells records afford additional evidence of his interest in humanity; they also demonstrate the value he finds in concrete, particular experience. The particular facts of a street scene have, for Howells, their own kind of splendor. Moreover, his delight hardly surpasses that felt by the reader, who considers the moments spent in viewing these slight scenes among the best moments. The dramatic encounters have a curious completeness in their inconclusiveness, and suggest that Howells knew quite well that small particulars can do fine service in dramatizing the romance of real life.

The benefits one accrues from having traveled with Howells are many. The reader is not likely to forget the delight of his first reading of *London Films.* When more objective, he can conclude that the qualities which Auden specifies as necessary to travel literature are qualities which Howells' books possess in admirable degree—meaning, relation, and importance. In volumes which are seemingly casual and light, Howells reveals his ability to extract significance from what Auden terms "historical personal events."

Howells' travel books deserve to be read with care, for they invite comparison with the work of Emerson, Hawthorne, and James. Howells works within a tradition of American travel writing but also contributes much to the tradition. His books on England differ from Emerson's *English Traits* in being less comprehensive and less philosophical, less direct, and less absolute in their conclusions. Howells has in common with Emerson an interest in organic form and symbolic values, but temperamentally he has more in common with Hawthorne. Both display a healthy skepticism, find humor in their personal encounters with Englishmen, and demonstrate a sympathy for those who suffer from unjust social conditions. With James, Howells shares a belief in the value of subjective response to immediate experience, and both writers render impressions in an attempt to verify reality. James' impressions more often treat visual experience; Howells' treat personal and social experience.

Howells demonstrates that even though the travel book records the surfaces and edges of life, it can in its modest way show some of the directions of man's soul. Howells' books reveal how much his travels were a part of his search for the real. He perceptively examines the travel genre in his reviews and devises techniques in his practice which can effectively treat the realities of travel. The formal requirements of travel literature challenged him, and he cared enough for the genre to meet successfully the challenge.

NOTES

1. W. D. Howells, "Editor's Easy Chair," *Harper's Monthly*, CXXVI (April 1913), 798.
2. *Ibid.*
3. *Ibid.*, p. 797.
4. *Ibid.*, p. 799.

BIBLIOGRAPHY

BOOKS

Cady, Edwin H. *The Realist at War: The Mature Years, 1885-1920, of William Dean Howells*. Syracuse: Syracuse University Press, 1958.

————. *The Road to Realism: The Early Years, 1837-1885, of William Dean Howells*. Syracuse: Syracuse University Press, 1956.

Carter, Everett. *Howells and the Age of Realism*. Philadelphia: J. B. Lippincott, 1954.

Cooke, Delmar Gross. *William Dean Howells: A Critical Study*. New York: E. P. Dutton and Company, 1922.

Dickinson, Emily. *The Complete Poems of Emily Dickinson*. Edited by Thomas H. Johnson. Boston: Little, Brown, and Company, 1960.

Eliot, T. S. "Tradition and Individual Talent," *The Great Critics: An Anthology of Literary Criticism*. Edited by J. H. Smith and E. W. Parks. Third edition. New York: W. W. Norton and Company, Inc., 1961.

Emerson, Ralph Waldo. *English Traits*. Boston: Phillips, Sampson, and Company, 1856.

————. *Selections from Ralph Waldo Emerson: An Organic Anthology*. Edited by Stephen Whicher. Boston: Houghton Mifflin Company, 1960.

Firkins, Oscar. *William Dean Howells: A Study*. Cambridge: Harvard University Press, 1924.

Fryckstedt, Olov W. *In Quest of America: A Study of Howells' Early Development as a Novelist*. Upsala, Sweden: 1958.

Gibson, William M. and George Arms. *A Bibliography of William Dean Howells*. New York: New York Public Library, 1948.

Hawthorne, Nathaniel. *Our Old Home and English Note-Books*. Vol. VII of *The Works of Nathaniel Hawthorne*. Edited by George Parsons Lathrop. 15 vols. Boston: The Riverside Press, 1891.

Howells, Mildred (ed.). *Life in Letters of William Dean Howells*. 2 vols. Garden City, New York: Doubleday, Doran, and Company, Inc., 1928.

Howells, William Dean. *Certain Delightful English Towns*. New York: Harper and Brothers, 1906.

————. *Familiar Spanish Travels*. New York: Harper and Brothers, 1913.

————. *Indian Summer*. Introduction by William M. Gibson. New York: E. P. Dutton and Company, 1958.

————. *Italian Journeys*. New York: Hurd and Houghton, 1867.

————. *Italian Journeys*. New and Enlarged Edition. Boston: J. R. Osgood and Company, 1872.

————. *A Little Swiss Sojourn*. New York: Harper and Brothers, 1892.

————. *London Films*. New York: Harper and Brothers, 1906.

————. *Roman Holidays and Others*. New York: Harper and Brothers, 1908.

————. *Seven English Cities*. New York: Harper and Brothers, 1909.

————. *A Traveler from Altruria*. Introduction by Howard Mumford Jones. New York: Sagamore Press, 1957.

————. *Tuscan Cities*. Boston: Ticknor and Company, 1886.

————. *Venetian Life*. Second edition. New York: Hurd and Houghton, 1867.

————. *Venetian Life*. New and Enlarged Edition. Boston: J. R. Osgood and Company, 1872.

————. *Venetian Life*. 2 vols. Boston: Houghton, Mifflin and Company, 1891.

————. *William Dean Howells: Representative Selections*. Edited by Clara Marburg Kirk and Rudolf Kirk. Revised edition. New York: Hill and Wang, 1961.

James, Henry. *The American Scene*. Edited by W. H. Auden. New York: Charles Scribner's Sons, 1946.

————. *The American Scene*. Edited by Leon Edel. Bloomington: Indiana University Press, 1968.

————. *English Hours*. Edited by Alma Louise Lowe. Second edition. London: W. Heineman, 1960.

————. *Italian Hours*. New York: Grove Press, Inc., 1959.

Kirk, Clara Marburg. *W. D. Howells and Art in His Time*. New Brunswick, N.J.: Rutgers University Press, 1965.

Matthiessen, F. O. *American Renaissance*. New York: Oxford University Press, 1962.

Smith, Henry Nash. *Mark Twain: The Development of a Writer*. Cambridge: Harvard University Press, 1962.

Strout, Cushing. *The American Image of the Old World.* New York: Harper and Row, 1963.

Tocqueville, Alexis de. *Democracy in America.* 2 vols. New York: Random House, 1962.

Woodress, James. *Howells & Italy.* Durham, N.C.: Duke University Press, 1952.

Wright, Nathalia. *American Novelists in Italy.* Philadelphia: University of Pennsylvania Press, 1965.

PERIODICALS

Arms, George. "Howells' English Travel Books: Problems in Technique," *PMLA,* LXXXII (March, 1967), 104-16.

[Howells, William Dean.] "Editor's Easy Chair," *Harper's Monthly,* CXXVI (April, 1913), 796-99. (Review of Arnold Bennett's *Your United States.*)

————. "Editor's Study," *Harper's Monthly,* LXII (January, 1886), 321-26. (Brief mention of the sketches by Pennell which appear in *Tuscan Cities.*)

————. "Editor's Study," *Harper's Monthly,* LXXV (September, 1887), 638-42. (On democracy in literature.)

————. "A New Observer," *Atlantic Monthly,* XLV (June, 1880), 848-49. (Review of J. B. Harrison's *Certain Dangerous Tendencies in American Life.*)

————. "Recent Literature," *Atlantic Monthly,* XXXVI (July, 1875), 113-15. (Review of Henry James, *Transatlantic Sketches.*)

————. "Recent Travels," *Atlantic Monthly,* XXIV (August, 1869), 250-60. Reviews of Charles Carleton Coffin's *Our New Way Round the World;* Richard Henry Dana's *Two Years Before the Mast;* A. K. McClure's *Three Thousand Miles Through the Rocky Mountains;* and Alfred Russell Wallace's *The Malay Archipelago.*)

————. "Review of W. Pembroke Fetridge's *Harper's Hand-Book for Travellers in Europe and the East,*" *Atlantic Monthly,* XIX (March, 1867), 380-83.

————. "Review of Nathaniel Hawthorne's *Italian Note-Books,*" *Atlantic Monthly,* XXIX (May, 1872), 624-26.

————. "Review of John Hay's *Castilian Days,*" *Atlantic Monthly,* XXVIII (November, 1871), 636-38.

————. "Review of Bayard Taylor's *By-Ways of Europe,*" *Atlantic Monthly,* XXIII (June, 1869), 764-65.

————. "Review of Charles Dudley Warner's *Mummies and Moslems,*" *Atlantic Monthly,* XXXVIII (July, 1876), 108-12.

————. "Reviews of Henry W. Bellows' *The Old World in its New Face: Im-*

pressions of Europe in 1867-68 and John Durand's translation of *Italy, Rome, and Naples, from the French of Henri Taine," Atlantic Monthly,* XXII (June, 1868), 124-27.

[James, Henry.] "Review of William Dean Howells' *Italian Journeys,*" *North American Review,* CVI (January, 1868), 336-39.

Jovanovich, William. "The Misuses of the Past," *Saturday Review,* April 2, 1966, pp. 21-24.

Pennell, Joseph. "Adventures of an Illustrator: With Howells in Italy," *Century,* CIV (May, 1922), 135-41.

Warren, Robert Penn. "A Lesson Read in American Books," *The New York Times Book Review,* December 11, 1955, Sec. 7, pp. 1, 33.

UNPUBLISHED MATERIALS

Carrington, George Cabell, Jr. "William Dean Howells as a Satirist." Unpublished dissertation, Ohio State University, Columbus, 1959. (Ann Arbor, Michigan: University Microfilms, Inc., 1961.)

Daniel, Maggie Browne. "A Study of William Dean Howells' Attitude Toward and Criticism of the English and Their Literature." Unpublished dissertation, University of Wisconsin, Madison, 1953.

Dowling, Joseph Albert. "William Dean Howells and his Relationship with the English: A Study of Opinion and Literary Reputation." Unpublished dissertation, New York University, New York, 1957. (Ann Arbor, Michigan: University Microfilms, Inc., 1958.)

Stiles, Marion Lumpkin. "Travel in the Life and Writings of William Dean Howells." Unpublished dissertation, University of Texas, Austin, 1946.

INDEX

Alhambra, the, Spain, 126
America: democracy in, 55; nature in, 94; houses in, 100; true spirit of, 112; morality in, 115; millionaires in, 117; lack of a past of, 119
American character: contrasted to English, 96, 97; mentioned, 63, 81
American Renaissance, 97
American Scene, The (James), 1, 91
Anglican Church, 103
Architecture: of Renaissance, 39, 40; Howells' reluctance to criticize, 39, 84; and function, 70, 71; and nature, 95, 96; Greek, 120.
Arms, George: on Howells' techniques, 80-81, 85, 106n2, 107n25; mentioned, 76n10
Arrighi, Bartolomeo, 36
Art: Hawthorne on, 7; Howells' judgments about, 7-8; social obligations of, 41-42, 53-54; Howells' attitudes about, in *Tuscan Cities*, 68; Howells and French Impressionists, 68; human element in, 70, 71, 73; imaginative spirit of, 72; baroque, 119;

and "romanticistic" sculpture, 111; conclusions about, in *Roman Holidays*, 120. *See also* names of individual artists and works
Art criticism: deficiencies of, 7-8, 39-40, 71-72, 120, 132; anti-intellectualism of Howells' attitudes about, 8; and artist's motives, 72-73
Auden, W. H., 1, 133
Aurelius, Marcus, 115

Bandini, 53
Baroque art, 119
Basque country, Spain, 122-23
Bath, England, 95, 103, 104
Bellows, Henry W., 9n8
Bennett, Arnold, 130, 131
Books (Howells). *See Certain Delightful English Towns, Criticism and Fiction, Familiar Spanish Travels, Indian Summer, Italian Journeys, The Leatherwood God, A Little Swiss Sojourn, London Films, A Modern Instance, The Rise of Silas Lapham, Roman Holidays, Seven*

139